I0762856

RENAISSANCE OF A BOSS

Also by Rick Ross with Neil Martinez-Belkin

Hurricanes: A Memoir

The Perfect Day to Boss Up: A Hustler's Guide to Building Your Empire

RICK ROSS

WITH NEIL MARTINEZ-BELKIN

RENAISSANCE OF A BOSS

NOTES FROM A CREATIVE REAWAKENING

HANOVER
SQUARE
PRESS

Recycling programs for this product may not exist in your area.

ISBN-13: 978-1-335-00759-9

Renaissance of a Boss

Hanover Square Press
22 Adelaide St. West, 41st Floor
Toronto, Ontario M5H 4E3, Canada
HanoverSqPress.com

HarperCollins Publishers
Macken House, 39/40 Mayor Street Upper,
Dublin 1, D01 C9W8, Ireland
www.HarperCollins.com

Printed in U.S.A.

26 27 28 29 30 LBC 5 4 3 2 1

RENAISSANCE OF A BOSS

TABLE OF CONTENTS

RENAISSANCE

re·nais·sance *noun*

a movement or period of vigorous artistic and intellectual activity

CHAPTER 1

MY CREATIVE RUT

I WAS JUST GETTING BACK FROM MY MORNING walk when my sister called. Renee always hits me up around that time. She'll give me any updates from the day before and and remind me of what's on my agenda for the day ahead.

The head of the book publisher had reached out. They were putting another deal on the table.

I wasn't surprised: I don't claim to be an expert on the economics of book publishing, but I do know a thing or two about business. In the music industry, if a new artist came into the game and dropped two hit records back-to-back, no label on earth was going to drop them. Over the past few years, I'd delivered two instant *New York Times* bestsellers, basically the equivalent of hitting the *Billboard* 200 charts. By every metric, my two books had been a great success for all parties involved. So it only made sense that they were opening their checkbook to try to convince Rozay to give them a third.

I liked the offer. Numbers wise, they came correct. But more than that, I had enjoyed the experience of working on my first two books. The way my brain is wired, I'm not naturally inclined to introspection. I don't spend a whole lot of time going down memory lane, reflecting on how I got to where I'm at or why I made the moves that I did. I've always been more of a forward thinker. I'm usually trying to figure out what the next play is. That's just how I operate. But writing a book required me to exercise different muscles in my mind. I found that process to be intellectually stimulating.

I sent Renee back to them with a counteroffer. If they doubled up on the money, we could make it a two-book deal. She called me back later that afternoon. No further negotiations would be needed. A formal contract was being drafted and was en route for signature by the end of the week. We had ourselves a deal.

Abracadabra.

Just like that, I was on the hook for two more books. My shit was about to be a whole damn series. Fuck Harry Potter. Rozay was coming for his spot. His hocus-pocus-looking ass had a lightning bolt on his forehead, but I had the state of Florida tatted on mine. I'm talking about Dade County. 305. M.I. Yayo.

The moment called for celebration. I popped a bottle of my favorite sparkling wine—Luc Belaire Luxe, of course—and poured myself a glass. I reached for a joint and sparked it up. I took a deep inhale and closed my eyes. In my mind, I could already see the future collector's edition boxed set of all my books lined up together. I envisioned all the high-end details and special effects. The bold, gold foil–embossed font on the main title. The spot gloss on the smaller lettering. I considered different design options for the endpapers. I could keep it classic and just have it be the Maybach Music Group logo, or I could get whimsical with this shit and have it be a wallpaper-like pattern of pears. Shout out to all the pear. If you know, you know. I may even include one of those built-in ribbon bookmarks I'd seen before in other books. Why not? The possibilities were endless. But one thing was certain: I wanted the whole package to be stunning. Breathtaking.

The part that was not immediately clear to me was what my next book would be about. My literary debut, *Hurricanes*, had been my origin story. A straight-up autobiography. It told the story of my come-up in Carol City and my subsequent rise to becoming the biggest boss of the rap game. Two years later, I released *The Perfect Day to Boss Up: A Hustler's Guide to Building Your Own Empire.* That was more of a business book. It resonated with folks who weren't even necessarily die-hard fans of my music but were intrigued by my success as an entrepreneur and inspired by my hustle.

So, what was supposed to come next? I wasn't sure.

I called up my coauthor, Neil.

"You hear we're writing a third book?"

"I did get a call about that," Neil said. "Look, you know I love working together, but what would a third book even be about? What do you feel like you have left to say?"

"Ain't that your job to figure out?"

"Fair. I'll come down and we'll see what we can come up with."

I called my sister back.

"Did they say what they want the book to be about?"

"Will, you know I don't know nothing about that. That's for you and Neil to figure out. I just asked the man about the money." She paused. "Now that I think of it, I do think he suggested something about creativity."

A book about creativity. On its face, it wasn't a bad idea. I liked the general concept. After all, I'm most definitely a highly creative individual. I could see the appeal in me pulling back the curtains and giving my readers an inside look into my creative process. I had some gems to drop, some sage words of wisdom to impart. That would make for a compelling read. But I also knew that might be a challenging book to write.

Creativity is an imprecise science—at least, for me it is. There are best practices and major keys to success—shout-out to my brother DJ Khaled—but there is also some mystery involved. Creativity doesn't follow step-by-step rules like math or business. That stuff is logical; if this, then that. It's a structured, linear way of thinking about things.

Logic does play a role in the creative process, but so does lateral thinking. Lateral thinking is where elements like intuition, imagination, and risk-taking come into play. Those things can appear to be in direct opposition to logic.

The creative process is full of these types of paradoxes. As I started brainstorming ideas for the book, I realized that every point I came up with had an equally valid counterpoint. How could I make the claim, for example, that creativity springs from diligent preparation and hard work, but then turn around and acknowledge the divine intervention that takes place when a genius idea strikes you out of nowhere like that lightning bolt on Harry Potter's head?

How could I stress the importance of coming up with a game plan and sticking to a consistent daily routine, but at the same time tell someone to be ready to throw the plan out the window and shake shit up if things start to feel stale?

How could I recommend apprenticeship and following in the footsteps of the greats that came before you, but also say to be an original and develop your own creative identity?

Intuitively, I understood these things were all two sides of the same coin. The yin and yang. But in written form, I wondered if I would come across as a hypocrite who was constantly contradicting himself.

But there was a bigger issue with this book idea. I knew if I tried, I could probably figure out how to explain the paradoxes that exist within the creative process. As a matter of fact, I think I just did a pretty decent job of that in the last few paragraphs. The real problem with me writing a book about creativity was that I was going through something. Something I had never experienced before. I hadn't shared it with anyone, and I barely understood it myself.

Maybe I was having a midlife crisis. According to the internet, all the telltale symptoms of one were there. I *was* approaching fifty years of age. I *was* questioning my life's purpose. I *had* been buying a lot of sports cars lately. Actually, scratch that last one. The buying cars shit was nothing new for me.

So what was really going on? On paper, I had nothing to frown about. From the outside looking in, things could not have been going better for me. As an artist, I'd accomplished damn near every goal I'd set for myself. I had a Platinum-selling album to my name. Several more Gold ones. I had a catalog of music I was proud of. In the boom-or-bust world of entertainment, so far, my work had stood the test of time. I had traveled the world and performed my music in front of sold-out stadiums in countries I'd never even heard of growing up. And I'd been able to pay my success forward. As the CEO of Maybach Music Group, I was blessed to have a hand in the development of artists like Wale, Meek Mill, and French Montana, along with many others. I'd cemented a legacy in hip-hop as one of the best. One of the greats.

My endeavors outside music had been just as impressive. I'd found success in real estate, fast-food franchising, wine and spirits, and book publishing, just to name a few. I was a nine-figure nigga. I had achieved financial freedom and secured the generational wealth I'd always dreamed of. I had obtained every object of my desire. I owned mansions in several states. A private jet. A yacht. Hundreds of cars. You get the idea.

But as I approached the twenty-year anniversary of my debut album, *Port of Miami*, for whatever reason, I was feeling uninspired. I was still keeping busy. I was booked for shows every weekend. But I had started to feel like I was just going through the motions. I recently purchased a Tesla Cybertruck and it has a self-driving feature on there called Supervised. It's autopilot. You switch on Supervised mode, type in your destination, and let the Cybertruck take it from there. It drives, it turns, it parks, and you just sit there, watching it all happen. That's what my life was feeling like. Like I had beaten a video game and now I was just going back and replaying the same old levels.

Music is an artform and art has no age limit. But it's also a sport, especially in hip-hop. So throughout my career I've approached my craft as an artist but also as a competitor. I started as an unproven prospect. Then I was an up-and-coming contender, fighting my way up the rankings. Eventually I became the undisputed heavyweight champion, and I defended my title for many years.

But like with most sports, hip-hop is a young man's game. My last album, *Richer Than I Ever Been*, had been well received, but it was also the lowest-selling and lowest-charting album of my career. I could argue that no artist is selling records like they were ten years ago, and that would be true. The industry has most definitely changed. But it was also true that I was no longer competing for that number one spot, and it was time for me to pass the torch to the next generation.

I still loved making music. I never lost my passion for that. But I may have lost that sense of urgency that had pushed me for all those years. Hunger, ambition, and a competitive spirit can be big motivating factors for creative people. Money, success, and comfort can have the opposite effect. It had been months since I'd felt the urge to go to the studio. That was very unlike me.

All of this could only mean one thing: I was in the midst of my first creative rut.

And now I had just signed on to write a book about creativity—at a time when I wasn't sure if I had anything left to say and was feeling more unimaginative than I could ever remember. The irony of that was not lost on me. There was no way I was going to pay the publisher back the advance. I don't leave money on the table. But it had been a minute since I'd put on my author hat. Was I about to experience writer's block?

CHAPTER 2

GROUNDHOG DAY

I MAY BE THE BIGGEST BOSS THAT YOU'VE seen thus far, but I'm still a human being. The fact that I'm rich, famous, and extremely good-looking doesn't exempt me from feelings of apathy and boredom. As glamorous as my life is, I know how it feels to be stuck in a repetitive cycle, where you find yourself doing the same shit day after day. There are only so many times you can fly private before the initial novelty of it starts to fade and it's just another part of that cycle. It felt clear that the monotony of daily life had some part in the creative slump I was experiencing.

Everything I was doing felt too easy. In fact, "it's too easy" had become my catchphrase, only it used to be a flex. Every day I get presented with all sorts of different offers. Show bookings from concert promoters. Feature requests from record labels. Endorsement deals. If the price was right and it wasn't a bad look, I'd tell them, "It's too easy," and hang up the phone. Whatever it was would get added to my calendar and I wouldn't think about it again until it was time for me to go do whatever it was I had agreed to do.

But it had gotten to a point where "it's too easy" was starting to feel more like a problem. Show up. Do the thing. Get the money. Repeat. *It was all too easy.*

Have you seen the 1993 film *Groundhog Day*? That shit is a classic. Bill Murray stars as Phil Connors, a jaded TV weatherman who gets sent to the small town of Punxsutawney, Pennsylvania, to cover its annual Groundhog Day celebration. At the start of the movie, Phil is a cynical asshole. His whole attitude and outlook on life are nothing but negative. He puts in a half-assed effort at his job and then retires to his hotel room for the night, eager to leave the bumblefuck town first thing in the morning. But when he wakes up, something strange has happened. It's Groundhog Day again. Phil finds himself stuck in a time loop where he is forced to relive the events of February 2 over and over and over again.

At the beginning of the film, Phil uses the time loop to indulge in hedonistic pleasures. Knowing he won't have to face consequences for his actions, he engages in all types of depraved debauchery and scumbag behavior. He drinks and drives. He manipulates women. He eats cake for breakfast. This motherfucker even robs an armored truck.

Eventually Phil crashes out. Big-time. Once he hits rock bottom he has no choice but to confront the emptiness of his existence. As the movie progresses, we see him undergo a transformation. He starts to use his days to better himself. He learns to play the piano and becomes fluent in French. He masters the art of ice sculpting. Most importantly, he starts to use his inside knowledge of future events to help out others. In the end, Phil becomes a better and much happier person, with a newfound appreciation for his life.

Groundhog Day was marketed as a romantic comedy, but that label doesn't do it justice. It's a deep film. It's about the meaning of life. How those repetitive cycles we all find ourselves trapped in can provide space for us to become better people. Our capacity to grow and experience personal transformation even in the most mundane circumstances. I highly recommend it. It's very uplifting.

I've met Bill Murray, by the way. And not only have I met Bill Murray, but I've hit the studio with Bill Murray. Believe it or not, there is an unreleased Rick Ross and Bill Murray collaboration sitting on a hard drive and gathering dust in a drawer somewhere. Don't ask me where it's at. It's in Bill's possession.

This was maybe ten years ago. At the time, Bill was putting together a Christmas movie for Netflix titled *A Very Murray Christmas*. He had written the script alongside his longtime friend and collaborator Mitch Glazer, a mutual friend of ours. A couple years back, Mitch had written a part for me in an episode of *Magic City*, a series he created for Starz that takes place in 1950s Miami. I got to play the role of bolita boss "Butterball," the owner of an illegal gambling house. It was my acting debut, and I had a great time doing it, especially because I had been a fan of the show's first season.

So when Mitch hit me about the Bill Murray project, I was excited to get involved. I linked up with Bill, Mitch, and comedian Paul Shaffer at a recording studio in Philadelphia. We chopped it up and they explained that *A Very Murray Christmas* was a Christmas musical comedy, and they had a part for me in one of the last scenes. In what would be a dream sequence, Bill and I would perform a rendition of Albert King's 1974 song "Santa Claus Wants Some Lovin'." I was familiar with the song. Albert King was from Indianola, Mississippi, which is only an hour away from Clarksdale, the city where I was born. Albert King was one of the legendary "Three Kings of the Blues," alongside B.B. King and Freddie King.

Bill had already recorded his part of the song. They played it for me a couple of times and I understood the assignment. I hopped into the booth and knocked out my part. We shared a few more laughs and then all went our separate ways, with plans to film the scene for the movie a couple weeks later.

Unfortunately, that didn't end up happening. Something came up on my end and I couldn't make it on the day of the shoot. I learned a valuable lesson that day. As it turns out, movie productions work on extremely tight schedules. They wouldn't be able to make accommodations for Rozay. A few months later, Bill put me on blast during an appearance on *Jimmy Kimmel Live!* when he was asked about our upcoming collaboration.

"He came and recorded the song and that was the last we saw of him. He didn't show up to shoot the song. So, if anyone out there sees a three-hundred-pound guy who looks like he was supposed to be in New York two weeks ago, let me know."

When *A Very Murray Christmas* released later that year, I found out that George Clooney had stepped in for me. You think I'm joking? Go pull it up on Netflix right now. This is an irrefutable fact: I was offered a role in a major motion picture, and when I was unable to fulfill that role, George Clooney was the actor they selected to play my part. I'm talking about the winner of two Academy Awards and four Golden Globes, a two-time winner of *People* magazine's "Sexiest Man Alive." If that alone doesn't prove to you that Rozay is a global sex symbol, I don't know what else to tell you. You must just be a hater.

Maybe you're surprised I said yes to doing a Netflix Christmas movie in the first place. And that's exactly my point: acting is not my forte. Having a director tell me what to do and what to wear and how to deliver words is most definitely outside my comfort zone.

But as a rule, I always want to say "yes" whenever I get an opportunity to try something new. In this case, I said yes to playing in Mitch Glazer's "Butterball"—which led me to the opportunity to work with Mitch again and be in Bill Murray's movie. Sure, I ended up folding on this particular opportunity, but it still proves my point: when things feel too easy, do something outside of your comfort zone. If I hadn't flaked out on Bill Murray, you already know I would have name dropped him in at least once in one of my rhymes.

I know what some of you are thinking: "Rozay, I'm stuck at my nine-to-five job. I don't have the luxury of being able to go kick it with Bill Murray whenever I need a change of scenery." I hear that. I recognize I'm able to travel to new places and try out new things more than the average person.

But let me offer a rebuttal. You don't always need to do something drastic to break up the monotony of your work. Sometimes, it's just taking what's already there and changing the little details. You never know what the result might be.

Here's an example. Every now and then I get booked for a private event where I'm asked to keep my cursing to a minimum. Maybe it's a corporate event or a Bar Mitzvah or a Sweet Sixteen. Some shit like that. Those types of bookings usually pay so well that I'm happy to oblige those requests. In those cases, I recite the clean lyrics to "Hustlin'" that I recorded back in the day in order to get the song serviced to radio.

> Who ~~the fuck~~ **you suckas** think you ~~fuckin~~' **trippin'** with?
> **Yes**, I'm the ~~fuckin'~~ boss
> 745, white-on-white, that's ~~fuckin'~~ **Rick** Ross

As you can see, "that's fuckin' Ross" becomes "that's Rick Ross." One day, for some reason, I spontaneously said Ricky instead of Rick. And I realized I liked the sound of that way better, even more than the explicit version. Adding that extra syllable and that high-pitched "ee" sound to the end of "Rick" made for a higher inflection point before the beat comes crashing back down and I say "Ross." The contrast made it hit even harder. Now, whenever I perform "Hustlin'," I say "Ricky," regardless of whether or not I'm cursing that night.

Another example: "Pop That," my double-Platinum smash with French Montana, Drake, and Lil Wayne. That's another record that always goes off at my shows. I've got a line on it that goes:

> Film it, film it, this bitch want me to film it
> Ballin', ballin' like I play for New England

Even though they're the Dolphins' AFC East rivals, I'm a fan of the Patriots. How can you not respect the dynasty that Bob Kraft, Bill Belichick, and Tom Brady built? But not everybody feels that way. The Patriots are a polarizing team. So depending on the city I'm performing in, I can swap out "New England." If I'm in Atlanta, I can say "the Falcons." Or If I'm in Baltimore, I can say "the Ravens." But I can't do it everywhere. It has to work. For one, the name of the city or its team has to match up with the three-syllable structure of the line before, which is "to film it." "Ballin', ballin' like I play for the Browns" just doesn't sound right. And the team has to actually have a winning record, or it won't resonate with the crowd, so the Browns wouldn't make sense on that level either.

Either way, you get the point: shake up the details, even if you have to work a little to make it fit. The same way the monotony of a nine-to-five job in a cubicle becomes mind-numbing? That can happen with creative work, too. When it does, try to find those small, subtle ways you can refresh the things that have gotten stale.

Before my shows, I'll run through my setlist with my DJ and look for any little adjustments to make this one a little different from the last. If you're not paying close attention, you might think I just do the same exact performance every weekend. But I'm always looking for small ways I can go out and improve on what I do best.

I get instant feedback on these little changes, too: when I hit the stage, I pay attention to the crowd and how they react to those different choices I've made. When I pull something off and the whole room goes crazy, those moments are priceless. It's why I still love hitting the road and performing my music all these years later.

CHAPTER

3

YOUR CREATIVE IDENTITY

FRESH OUT OF IDEAS, I DECIDED TO EXPERIment with some magic mushrooms.

Aside from weed, I've never really messed with drugs. I'm not a big fan of narcotics. I had a brief stint of sipping lean back in the day, but I wouldn't recommend that poison to anyone, especially if you're trying to plant seeds of creativity and fuel your imagination. If anything, that shit is a creativity killer.

I believe there's a common misconception when it comes to creativity and drugs. Motherfuckers hear "Purple Haze" one time and start thinking if they drop acid they'll be able to play the guitar like Jimi Hendrix or write a song like "Lucy in the Sky with Diamonds" like John Lennon and George Harrison. It doesn't work like that. Those motherfuckers were who they were long before the drugs kicked in, and they were who they were long after the effects wore off.

In my younger days, I was around a lot of coke and dope, but I never touched any of that junk myself. I saw firsthand the destructive effects those drugs had on people's lives and their communities. For every great creation that may have been slightly influenced by drugs or alcohol, there are a hundred motherfuckers who crashed out in devastating fashion.

Now that I've gotten my D.A.R.E. public service announcement out of the way, let me tell you about these magic mushrooms I took.

According to the New York Academy of Sciences, the term "psychedelic" was coined in 1957 by a British psychiatrist by the name of Humphry Osmond. This was back when motherfuckers were still being named Humphry. I can't believe women were really giving birth, looking down at their newborn baby for the first time, and thinking to themselves, *That's Humphry.*

Anyway, Humphry was looking for a word that captured the mind-expanding effects and altered states of consciousness brought on by substances like LSD and mescaline, the psychoactive compound derived from the peyote cactus. Previously these had been known as hallucinogens, but Humphry believed the term held a negative connotation that implied the effects were false perceptions. So, drawing from ancient Greek texts, he combined two words: *psyche*—which means "mind" or "soul"—and *dēlos*—which means "to manifest" or "make visible." The term "psychedelic" was born.

Unlike coke, dope, and amphetamines, psilocybin—the psychoactive compound in shrooms—is a nonaddictive, naturally occurring substance that comes from the earth. It's known for boosting creativity and opening doors to help people think outside the box. Considering the creative rut I was in, the idea of a transformative psychedelic experience was highly appealing.

On this particular occasion, I ingested the shrooms

at my Promise Land estate. At first, everything was cool. Thirty minutes in, I started to feel a tingling sensation in my hands and feet. The psychedelics were kicking in. I looked down at my hands and started to analyze the lines on my palms. What would a fortune teller have to say if they traced these lines? What story did they tell? I was mesmerized by the intricate, maze-like patterns of my fingertips. I turned my palm over. What was all the faded black ink that covered the back of my hands? A flood of memories of tattoo sessions and what was going on in my life at those times rushed into my mind. I hadn't thought of those things in years.

My state of heightened consciousness extended past my own physical form. I stepped out onto my balcony and took in the endless expanse of nature around me. Everything appeared brighter and more vivid. When I looked at a tree, it was like I could see every individual leaf swaying with the wind. Each one was a living, breathing form of life. I stared up at the sky, in awe of its scale and beauty. I was just a speck on this three-hundred-acre estate, which was just a speck on this earth, which was just a speck on God's universe. What did that mean? Was my existence meaningless? Was I really the biggest boss?

I remembered the book and got a hold of myself before I went too far down into the rabbit hole I was starting to head down. The meaning of life could wait. For now, I needed to narrow my focus. The creative process. What did I have to say about the creative process?

I mentioned this earlier, but I don't spend a lot of time thinking about why I am the artist I am, or how my art came to be what it is. I was just out here creating. I was just doing me. There was not a lot of self-analysis. But after some mushroom-induced reflection, I realized I did have a couple thoughts.

If you're feeling stuck and uninspired, a little self-awareness can go a long way. Knowing who you are is a good place to start when you're trying to figure out what to do.

My creative identity is an amalgamation of the two different worlds that shaped me as an artist and as a human being. I'm talking about the two different worlds that exist within Miami. The glitz and glamour of South Beach, and then the gritty and grimy side that's just over the MacArthur Causeway bridge. My music has always been a product of these two places.

I was not the first rapper to explore Miami's underbelly. Trick Daddy was rapping about street life in Liberty City's Pork & Beans projects before I came into the game. And I was not the first artist to paint a picture of the fast-paced and flashy lifestyle of Miami's rich and famous. But nobody had captured and blended both worlds into one the way I did.

I was able to pull this off because I had a unique level of exposure to both worlds. On the one hand, I'd sold nickel bags of crack in the Matchbox Projects of Carol City. But I'd also seen big money. I grew up around some of the biggest dope boys of that era, like Michael

Delancy and Wayne Parker. I'd seen Big Mike's gold 500 SEL Mercedes-Benz with the windshield wipers on the headlights. I'd seen Wayne Parker's mansion by Joe Robbie Stadium with a line of big body Benzes parked out front, and there was Wayne, walking out of that house in a silk robe sipping on a glass of champagne.

I was influenced by seeing those things. All those experiences and images fused together to form what became my creative DNA. That DNA is the foundation for everything I make.

As a creative, there's what you want to convey, and then there's how you convey it. Every artist has their own delivery method. A rapper like Nas takes a journalist-like approach, unfolding his stories scene by scene. Then you've got someone like J. Cole, whose verses can read like a diary entry. He tells you how he *feels*. When I think about my own music, more than anything I try to immerse you in a world. My verses are made up of a steady stream of details that pile up on top of each other. The narrative details aren't always crystal clear. Every bar may not have a direct connection to the one that preceded it. But altogether, the image that started in my mind always finds a unique way to emerge.

This is why I have songs like "Maybach Music" or "Aston Martin Music" or "Mafia Music" or "Cigar Music." I came up with the titles for those songs before I ever put pen to paper. I named them after hearing each beat. When J.U.S.T.I.C.E. League first played me the beat for what would become "Maybach Music," my initial thought was that it sounded expensive and luxurious. To me, it represented the feeling of being chauffeured around in a Maybach 57. With that image in mind, I got to work.

Years back, *DJBooth* published a list of the ten most luxurious Rick Ross records. In his article, writer Yoh Phillips wrote the following:

"The right collection of Ross' records will make a Honda Civic feel like a brand new Maybach; a one-bedroom apartment feel like a fully furnished Bel-Air mansion; payday feel like the direct deposit of a winning lottery ticket, and not a minimum wage check."

Shout-out to Yoh Phillips. I appreciated his kind words, but what I appreciated even more is that he understood what it is I do. As an artist, you hope people will like your work, but more than that, you want people to really *get* it.

Back to the shrooms. I had not yet resolved my existential crisis, but this was a start. Some introspection had occurred and I was pleased with that. At that point, I decided to give my mind a break and find something to watch on TV.

This is when everything started to go south. I can't tell you the amount of shrooms I took, but I can tell you with absolute certainty that I took too much. That was my first mistake. You've got to know what you're putting in your body. I hope my experience serves as a cautionary tale.

My second mistake—and this was the big one—was

that I decided to put on the 2022 historical thriller *Emancipation.*

From what I can remember, *Emancipation* is a good movie. Having said that, I would not recommend this film to any black man who's under the influence of psychedelics. For those that don't know, *Emancipation* stars Will Smith as Peter, a runaway slave attempting to make it to Baton Rouge after Abraham Lincon issues the Emancipation Proclamation. In short, the whole movie is Will Smith being chased by cruel slave catchers on horseback, along with their vicious attack dogs.

At first everything was cool. I was locked in and I remember thinking what a talented director Antoine Fuqua is and what a phenomenal actor Will Smith is. Will is an absolute legend. I didn't give a fuck that he had just slapped Chris Rock. I was only a few minutes into the movie, but I was already captivated by his performance. He deserved to win an Academy Award for this.

As the film progressed, my thoughts began to wander. Prior to his escape, Peter had been forced to work on building a railroad for the Confederacy. I got stuck on that. Who owned those railroad rights now? I needed to know. Because we were the ones who built them. So where was our back pay? Where was our equity in the railroad company? Who did I need to speak to about this? Was it the CEO of Amtrak or somebody else? In my mind, we owned the whole railroad system. We were entitled to it. I was livid. First thing in the morning, I was going to deal with this injustice, I told myself.

Just having to see Peter work on the railroads under those conditions had been deeply disturbing. But that was nothing compared to what I would soon be subjected to. The next thing I knew, I was seeing the heads of murdered slaves on poles and Peter's partners get eaten by alligators. This shit was too much. My thoughts began to spiral. This movie was not a good choice. I was way too fucked up to handle this right now. I began to sweat profusely. I could feel my heart pounding out of my chest.

I cut off the TV and headed to the bathroom. I had company that evening, so I asked her to run me a bath. I needed to calm my nervous system down and try to relax. I prayed a warm bath would do the trick.

While I waited for the bath to fill up, I got into the shower. I closed my eyes, hoping the darkness would quiet the chaos that was going on inside my mind. Standing under the water, feeling it against my skin, I remember thinking: *Why am I wet right now? Am I in the swamps with the alligators? Am I a runaway slave?*

I stumbled out of the shower and into the tub. This bath needed to work. I needed to turn these shrooms off. I wanted this to be over. And that's the last thing I remember.

When I opened my eyes, I saw the faces of five tall white men standing over me.

"William, are you okay?" one of them asked.

Damn, I thought. They got me.

CHAPTER

4

THE LIFE OF PABLO

DON'T WORRY. THE GROUP OF TALL WHITE men standing over me turned out to not be slave catchers. They were paramedics from the Southwest Ranches Fire Department. They'd been called to my home after I suffered a seizure in my bathtub.

As I began regaining consciousness and realized these Caucasian gentlemen meant me no harm, I noticed there were bubbles as far as my eyes could see. The bathtub had overflowed all the way into my bedroom.

Before things spiraled out of control, I'd had some good insights about my creative identity. But it was clear that a psychedelic-induced epiphany wasn't going to be the solution to my creative rut. I needed to go back to the drawing board.

A few weeks later I was inside the home of Gloria and Emilio Estefan. Look, I get a lot of love in Miami. I like to think that I'm something of a hometown hero. But if I were to tell you I was as beloved in this city as those two individuals, I would be pushing it. I'm talking about the Queen of Latin Pop. I'm talking about Miami Sound Machine. I'm talking about a hundred million records sold. I'm talking about "Come on, shake your body baby, do the conga." The Estefans are Miami royalty. The simple fact that I was standing inside their living room eating hors d'oeuvres was surreal. But it gets even crazier than that. The Estefans were my new next-door neighbors.

I had recently closed on the home of my dreams. I'd spent $37 million to become the proud owner of 37 Star Island, a six-bedroom waterfront mansion overlooking the aquamarine waters of Biscayne Bay. I hadn't moved in yet. There were major renovations in the works. But Gloria and Emilio, who live next door at number 39, were gracious enough to invite me over and welcome me to the community.

The Estefans have lived on Star Island for almost forty years, and you can see that history come through in their decor. Their home has character. It shares the story of their legendary lives. You can tell their furniture was acquired over years, and that they didn't just hire some interior designer to come in and pick out everything all at once. That stands out from the sterile feeling you find in a lot of celebrities' homes.

They also have an incredible collection of art. For real, their crib is like a museum. As the night went on, I kept returning to one particular piece: a blue crayon drawing of a naked woman lying on her back with a naked curly-headed man playing the flute standing next to her. Her nipples were depicted and so were his testicles. "Femme Couchee Et Flutiste." Lying Woman and Flutist. It was my first time seeing an original work of Pablo Picasso in the flesh.

Looking at an original piece of art in person is not the same as looking at a reproduced image of that piece of art. I have coffee table books that feature Picasso's paintings at my house. I follow accounts on social media that showcase his work. This was a different experience. When I first stopped to look, I backed up to several feet away. I wanted to take in the full effect. Then, I walked right up to the easel and leaned in so I could stare at it inches away from my face. I wanted to home in on all the small details. The texture of the paper. The direction of Picasso's crayon lines. I needed to better understand the mind of one of the most important and revolutionary artists in human history.

In addition to being incredibly talented, Picasso was also extremely prolific. His output was next level. Art historians have cataloged over twenty-six thousand pieces by him, and many believe his true number of works exceeds fifty thousand. The Estefans' piece was dated February 26, 1967, which meant Picasso was eighty-six at the time. He kept at it for many years after that.

Picasso worked up until the day he died. I'm not being hyperbolic. On the night before he passed, at ninety-one years of age, this motherfucker Pablo was up painting until three in the morning.

As far as work ethic goes, Pablo and I were cut from the same cloth. If he had been around to hear "Hustlin'," I know he would have seen himself in Rozay. But our processes were different. Mine is probably a bit more

meticulous. No disrespect to Pablo, but I would be surprised if it took him longer than five minutes to knock out that blue crayon piece.

That's not a judgment of the quality of his work. I'm just pointing out a difference in our methods. Some of the greatest rappers of all time take an approach that's more in line with Picasso's. Lil Wayne for example. Wayne is on the record saying he's recorded up to fifty-three songs in the same night.

During his renowned mixtape run of the mid-2000s, not only was Wayne knocking out songs at breakneck speed, but he was releasing all those joints to the public just as fast. He was dropping so much it was hard to keep up. If you didn't know better, it would be easy to assume his enormous quantity of music must have come at the expense of its quality. But you would be mistaken. You can't say that about Lil Wayne. Are there forgotten songs from that era? Of course. But when people talk about the heyday of Lil Wayne's career, they talk about Mixtape Weezy. They talk about his *Dedication* mixtape series with DJ Drama. They talk about *Da Drought*. They talk about *No Ceilings*. Many fans prefer the raw, unfiltered spontaneity you hear on his freestyles and mixtape cuts over his more polished studio albums.

On the other side of that spectrum, you'll find an artist like Dr. Dre. Dr. Dre has long been called the ultimate perfectionist. Dre has rejected that label, but I'm not buying it. This is a man who once said he hated *Straight Outta Compton*. He called it a rush job and said he "threw that thing together in six weeks so we could have something to sell out of the trunk."

He said these words about an album that is universally considered one of the greatest and most influential hip-hop records of all time. Anyone who's ever been in the studio with Dr. Dre knows that man is a perfectionist. I'm one of those people. I've seen it with my own two eyes.

The last time I worked with Dr. Dre was at his crib in the Brentwood neighborhood of Los Angeles. I believe the house previously belonged to Tom Brady. Dre built a ten-thousand-square-foot recording studio in the basement that rivals any top-of-the-line professional studio I've ever worked in. I can't even say it was in his basement. To describe this place with that word paints a picture that doesn't do it justice. It's an elaborate subterranean bunker. There were underground waterfalls and shit down there.

Dre invited me over to get involved in a top-secret project he was working on at the time. This was some fly shit. Dre had partnered up with Rockstar Games, a video game developer, to put together an album that would be released exclusively through *Grand Theft Auto*. In an upcoming update, *Grand Theft Auto Online: The Contract*, players would take on a mission that involved tracking down Dr. Dre's stolen cell phone before the thief leaked a batch of unreleased, never-before-heard Dre music to the world.

This was how Dre premiered and delivered his new body of work. Talk about thinking outside the box.

My contributions to the project were a couple of verses on a song called "The Scenic Route." I don't usually fly across the country to knock out guest verses, but Dr. Dre is not your average feature request. Not only that, this particular record required us to lock in the same studio. Dre wanted "The Scenic Route" to feature him and I rapping back and forth bar for bar. You know the style of rapping I'm talking about, right? Like Dre and Eminem did on "Guilty Conscience" or Jadakiss and Styles P on "We Gonna Make It."

When we were recording "The Scenic Route," Dre got stuck on his delivery of two words for what felt like an hour. I must have smoked five joints in the time it took him to lay down those two words exactly the way he wanted them to sound. I had to remind myself that this was Dr. Dre, and what a privilege it was for me to get a firsthand look at his process, regardless of how painstaking it was.

To his credit, Dr. Dre's catalog is damn near spotless. Again, some might argue that his extremely high standard for himself came at the expense of quantity. For as good as Dr. Dre's music is, I know we all wish he had more than three albums for us to enjoy. You can't help but wonder how much incredible unreleased music is sitting down there in Dre's underground bunker gathering dust.

When it comes to my own creative process, I fall somewhere between the two ends of the spectrum. I'm pretty detail oriented. Whether I'm picking beats, writing raps, or laying down vocals in the booth, I want everything to be perfect. I need each and every element to sound crisp and clear. After I'm done with a song, I typically go back and revisit it many times. If I'm working on an album, every song undergoes several rounds of tweaks and revisions over the course of months (sometimes even years) before it sees the light of day.

There's no right or wrong amount of creativity an artist needs to release to the world. It doesn't really matter if you create ten things in one day or take ten months to create one thing. Every artist is different.

What Picasso, Lil Wayne, Dr. Dre, and usually myself all share is that we all constantly create. At the end of the day, to be creative, you have to start somewhere. Sometimes people think it's the other way around. They wait around for lightning to strike. I'm sorry to break the bad news, but that's not the way it goes. It's engaging in the process of creation that ignites the imagination, and choosing to carry on no matter what your pace looks like.

The late, great Pablo Picasso said it best: "Inspiration exists, but it has to find you working." Pablo was right. I needed to get back to the basics and put the wheels in motion. The lightning strikes after you sit down and get to work.

CHAPTER

5

BOSS HABITS

IN THE FALL OF 2005, I RELEASED A SONG called "Hustlin'." After a decade of false starts and disappointing setbacks, my breakthrough moment finally arrived. "Hustlin'" was an immediate hit record and permanently altered the course of my life and career forever. I went from being broke and a complete unknown in the music industry to becoming the subject of a seven-figure major label bidding war.

At the time, it would have been easy to dismiss my success as dumb luck. Many people did. Everybody gets lucky once, right? I happened to be in the right place at the right time to stumble upon that undeniable beat, and then had a spontaneous moment of creative brilliance when I made the song.

That's not completely untrue. As I mentioned earlier, I do believe a higher power plays a part in our flashes of creative genius. God is the greatest, and I have to believe he made all the stars align for me on that particular day. He threw me an alley-oop. You can call it divine intervention. You can call it luck. However it is you want to acknowledge the miraculous invisible forces at play that are beyond our control.

But that's just one piece of the creative puzzle. The rest of the pieces are ones that *are* in your control. So allow me to tell you the rest of the story. Here's how I made "Hustlin'" happen:

I had spent a decade preparing myself for the moment when lightning struck. Ten years of waking up every day before the sun came up and going straight to the studio. Ten years of sitting in the studio writing raps for myself and others. When I first started out, I would write these never-ending raps that would span several pages in my rhyme book. With diligence, time, and practice, I learned how to package my verses into clean and concise sixteen-bar verses. I learned how to write hooks. I experimented with my voice in the booth and eventually landed on the deep, gravelly texture that you hear today.

I used to rap much faster than what you hear on "Hustlin'." But my intricate wordplay and rapid-fire delivery went over a lot of people's heads. Those complex rhyme schemes may have gone over better somewhere like New York, but in Miami, people were looking to have a good time. They weren't trying to solve my lyrical riddles. So I adapted.

Through daily practice, perseverance, and a lot of trial and error, I sharpened my skills and developed my creative identity. I eventually found my signature sound that emphasized commanding power over speed.

Then, I introduced it to the world with a simple,

clear, four-word message that anyone could understand: Every Day I'm Hustlin'.

Developing a consistent daily routine is essential to the creative process. Creativity aside, it's an overall life hack. When you start your day with a series of set rituals and habits, it creates momentum. Imagine if the only songs I ever made were the ones where I woke up that morning and had a great idea for a record in my mind. I wouldn't have much of a catalog under those conditions.

But by getting up and going to the studio, regardless of how I felt that morning or what else was on my mind, I was beginning the process of awakening my creative senses. When you already have a plan in place, you don't need to figure out the logistics of what to do next or where to start. That frees up space in your mind. It opens the door for the creative thoughts to enter.

The first thing I do when I wake up is go outside. I even have a name for my morning walks: "Barefoot Chronicles."

There are many benefits to starting your day by being in nature. Exposure to sunlight first thing in the morning can regulate your circadian rhythm—your body's internal clock—which is especially helpful for someone like me who has sleep issues.

Then there's the exercise part of my morning walks. Not only are there physical benefits—cardiovascular health, weight management, energy levels—it's also good for your mental health. Walking releases endorphins, which boost your mood, reduce stress, and improve your focus. Think about that. If your mood is low, your stress is high, and your thoughts are foggy, these are not ideal conditions to foster creative thinking. Like an athlete needs to stretch before they compete, a creator needs to prepare their mind before they create. My morning walks are an essential part of that preparation.

Personally, I like to walk barefoot. I want to feel the earth underneath my feet and the wet blades of grass between my toes. One of the perks of owning a three-hundred-acre estate is I can walk barefoot without having to worry about cutting myself on a shard of broken glass. My groundskeepers know my morning routine is sacred, and so they keep it pristine.

How do you start your day? Some people need a triple shot of espresso to wipe away the cobwebs. Some people jumpstart the senses with a cold plunge. Some people smoke a cigarette. Some people snort a line. Who am I to judge? By now it should come as no surprise that I bring a joint with me when I head out for my morning walk. For most people, this is not a productive way to start the day. But I'm not most people. Cannabis works for me. It provides me with a feeling of peace and helps me stay focused on my creative work amidst all the noise of my busy life.

If you follow me on social media, you may already be familiar with "Barefoot Chronicles." I'll sometimes document my walks on social media. But you should know those videos are almost always filmed at the very end of my walk, before I head back inside my house. The reason

I have so much to say in those videos is because I've just given myself thirty minutes to an hour of uninterrupted time in nature. The benefits of that are what you're seeing in "Barefoot Chronicles." By the time I'm winding down my walk, I'm usually bursting with new ideas.

Then it's usually time to go viral. Going viral on the internet is part of my morning routine. Sometime between the hours of 8:00 a.m. and 10:00 a.m. I'll hop on my Instagram Story and start talking shit. Sometimes I'll have leftover thoughts from my walk, but a lot of times I'll change the topic to something that I know will get people's attention and be reposted by the hip-hop blogs. Sometimes it's me chiming in on whatever the trending topic of the day is.

If it's a slow news day, I might just reignite an old feud with one of my adversaries. The topics may vary but some things remain the same. You will always see me holding a bottle of Luc Belaire. That way, when the blogs and aggregators repost whatever outlandish thing I decided to say that day, they will also be reposting my brands. It's called product placement. It's called free promotion. I'm a promotional juggernaut, what can I say?

The other thing that I do is bookend the videos with images advertising my own brands. So while I have your attention, I'm going to be sure to remind you that tickets are still available for the Rick Ross Car Show, and I'm also going to make sure you see this photo of Eddie Murphy holding up his signed copy of *Hurricanes*, which can be purchased wherever books are sold. If I see someone at an event, you better believe I'm shoving a bottle of Luc Belaire in their hand and having one of my homies snap a picture of it.

You get the idea: building a consistent routine can actually create space for the unexpected to happen. For example, I have a whole album in my camera roll dedicated exclusively to the types of marketing materials like the ones I mentioned above. And one day, while I was going about my usual "go viral" routine, I flipped through it looking for something to post.

I came across a screenshot dated December of 2021. It was a photograph I'd been tagged in by one of my fans. I had reposted it before. An Instagram account by the name of @bonadventureafrica had posted a photo of himself reading my book *The Perfect Day to Boss Up* from the top of Mount Kilimanjaro.

In that moment, something clicked in my mind.

I realized if I was going to write another book, I was going to have to find something really, truly new to talk about. Rozay making a lot more paper and buying a bunch of new whips wasn't going to cut it. This was bigger than the book. Those things weren't cutting it for *me* anymore. This was the reason for the slump that I was in. If I wanted to feel inspired and think differently, I had to do something different.

This was the answer. I was going to climb to the top of Mount Kilimanjaro. I needed to challenge myself. I needed to do something that didn't feel "too easy." I needed to push myself to the highest heights. What better way to do that than to climb the tallest mountain in Africa and the highest free-standing mountain in the world? I would document it all for the book. This would be my personal renaissance.

CHAPTER

6

NO IDEA'S ORIGINAL

No idea's original, there's nothing new under the sun
It's never what you do, but how it's done
What you base your happiness around? Material,
women and large paper?
That means you inferior, not major

—Nas, "No Idea's Original," *The Lost Tapes* (2002)

NAS IS, WITHOUT QUESTION, ONE OF HIP-hop's all-time greats. His gift for cinematic storytelling has already come up once in this book, and I can't guarantee you he won't come up again. I could spend a whole chapter praising Escobar's pen.

I was eighteen when Nas dropped his debut album, *Illmatic*. It was released on April 19, 1994, but if I remember correctly, it didn't reach my ears until sometime that summer. I had just graduated high school and was getting ready to head off to college in Georgia in the fall. Up to that point I had never traveled, other than the occasional road trip back to my birthplace of Clarksdale, Mississippi, to visit family. I'd never been to New York City, but when I listened to *Illmatic*, Nas took me there, to his Queensbridge housing projects. I could see the pictures he was painting. I felt like I was there.

Nas made the claim that no idea is original. And as if to prove his point, he wasn't even the first one to say *that*. That phrase is generally attributed to another one of the great storytellers in American history: Mark Twain, the author of *The Adventures of Tom Sawyer* and its sequel, *Adventures of Huckleberry Finn*. Mark Twain famously said that all ideas are secondhand.

> "There is no such thing as a new idea. It is impossible. We simply take a lot of old ideas and put them into a sort of mental kaleidoscope. We give them a turn and they make new and curious combinations. We keep on turning and making new combinations indefinitely; but they are the same old pieces of colored glass that have been in use through all the ages."

Nas also didn't come up with the bar *after* he raps "No idea's original"—"There's nothing new under the sun." Those words can be traced all the way back to Ecclesiastes 1:19 in the Bible, where they're attributed to King Solomon.

> *What has been is what will be*
> *And what has been done is what will be done;*
> *There is nothing new under the sun*

And it's not just the lyrics. The beat for "No Idea's Original" came from a producer by the name of the Alchemist. Many people, myself included, would call the Alchemist a true original. He's a hip-hop purist with a distinct style of beatmaking that is all his own. Having said that, "No Idea's Original" is also not even an original Alchemist beat. It's a sample flip of Barry White's 1973 song "I'm Gonna Love You Just a Little More Baby"—a record that has been sampled dozens of times before and after the Alchemist ever touched it. Shit, I even rapped over it on a song called "Even Deeper," on my 2010 mixtape *Ashes to Ashes.*

My point is this: every great idea is built upon ones that already exist. A creative act is when someone finds a way to connect and adapt those preexisting things to create a unique new thing the world has never seen before. That's what Nas did on the first two bars of "No Idea's Original." From there, he was off to the races. But his connection of those two first ideas was the spark that set everything off.

I wouldn't be the first person to climb Mount Kilimanjaro. I wouldn't be the first person to write a book about climbing Mount Kilimanjaro. But the biggest boss Rick Ross climbs Mount Kilimanjaro? Nobody had ever seen something quite like that before. And I'm willing to bet there aren't any books about climbing Mount Kilimanjaro where the author gets to talking about Picasso paintings and Bill Murray and shroom-induced seizures.

Nobody could tell me that wasn't a brilliant idea. I could see the book cover already. I would be sitting at the summit with a joint dangling from my mouth and a single teardrop streaming down my cheek. This was genius. I was a fucking creative genius.

CHAPTER 7

AGAINST DOCTOR'S ORDERS

MY SISTER CALLED. SHE WANTED TO KNOW how things were coming along with the book.

"I'm going to hike to the top of Mount Kilimanjaro," I told her, "and I'll write the book about that. Let's start putting everything together."

"You're doing what?"

When I told her that I wasn't joking, Renee was not amused. She did not like my idea. She had multiple concerns. First and foremost was my health and safety. The odds of me dropping dead on Mount Kilimanjaro were slim—less than 1 percent—but there was a much higher possibility of me becoming seriously ill and potentially having to get airlifted out of there. Of the thirty thousand people who attempt the climb each year, only about 60 percent end up reaching the summit. I could imagine the oddsmakers would give someone with my medical history and physique even less of a chance.

"That's what makes it exciting," I told her. "It's not 'too easy'!"

Renee was also having a hard time wrapping her mind around the fact that I would do something like this without an exorbitant bag of money involved. This trip was not the sort of thing the book publisher would foot the bill for.

At a minimum, I would need to block off two weeks for this trip. Probably more, depending on how much time I needed to recover after I got back. I thought it was unlikely that I would climb to the top of Kilimanjaro, fly home, and then be able to perform a show a few days later. That seemed like a recipe for disaster.

I could not remember the last time I took two weeks off. Neither could Renee. My sister is about business. She's not an artist, and I hadn't told her about the creative rut I was in. Before Renee started working with me full-time, she was an accountant. Her mind understands numbers. So she was looking at the amount of money I would miss out on by taking this trip, plus the amount of money that it would cost to finance it. She didn't like either of those numbers.

It wasn't like this trip would break the bank. I was in the best financial position I'd ever been. But I had just spent $30 million on my private jet and then immediately after that, I dropped another $37 million for my new crib on Star Island. The way my sister (and my banker) saw things, now was not the best time for me to take my foot off the gas and embark on some soul-searching journey.

There were bills to pay. We had to keep getting to the money.

"Will, why do you want to do this? There has got to be an easier way to get the book done."

"It's not even about the book," I tried to explain. I wanted to say this was about more than the book. That

I was stuck. I was in a rut, and this could be my ticket out. "I just—"

"Look, I'm going to schedule an appointment with your doctor. If he clears you to do it, we can talk about it more."

I have a history of seizures. To me, it's not a big deal. Once in a blue moon I have one, and afterward I wake up and I feel fine. Nine times out of ten I take a hit of my joint and carry on with my day. But I've come to learn that for the people who are around to witness my seizures, they are extremely traumatic events. I have opened my eyes to a lot of frightened faces hovering over me. So my family and my inner circle do not take it lightly. They are hypervigilant when it comes to making sure I take my prescribed medication twice a day.

Like I said, I don't feel like my seizures significantly impact my life. But the meds I take do come with some side effects, like fatigue and sleepiness. That's a problem for me. I have a very busy mind, and I live a very busy life, and I don't like taking anything that's going to slow me down. So Kilimanjaro aside, I was looking forward to meeting with my new neurologist. I had lost a few pounds and wanted to see about about lowering the dosage of my meds, because I was suspicious that my weight loss would result in more potent side effects. So I headed to the Emory Brain Health Center in Atlanta to try to get some answers.

"So when we saw you last year around this time," the doc said, "you were doing pretty good. How have you been doing since then?"

"I may have had a flash or two, but for the most part everything's been cool. The thing is, I've lost around twenty pounds, so I was thinking maybe we should reduce the dosage."

"Okay. So in some ways, what I want to do for you is simple. I want you to be seizure free, and I also want you to be side effect free from your medication. You mentioned you've had a few 'flashes.' Just so I'm clear, have you had any seizures since your last visit?"

"Yeah. I had a seizure in January."

"And was it your typical seizure?"

"It may have been a little unique."

"Any other recent seizures or just that one?"

"Just that one."

"And when you say it was unique . . . was there anything you think could have provoked it? Like forgetting to take your medicine or being sleep deprived?"

"That night I was partying a little differently."

"What do you mean by that?"

I know you're not supposed to withhold information from your doctor. I don't want to encourage anyone to do that. But I am a black man in the United States of America. I may be rich and have access to top medical professionals, but that doesn't erase the long history of systemic racism and discrimination that black folks have faced when it comes to healthcare. The Tuskegee experiments were not that long ago, and I'm from the South. The psychological effects of those things live on inside me too. This was also the first time I was meeting this particular doctor, who happened to be a white man. So forgive me if I wasn't entirely forthcoming about the whole shrooms-and-*Emancipation* ordeal that resulted in my most recent seizure.

"I'm sorry, what was your question?"

"I asked if there was anything in particular that might have provoked your seizure that night?"

"Just partying."

"Okay. So here are my thoughts. What matters to me is that you're not having seizures and that you feel good. It seems like for the most part, that's the case. So I'm hesitant to reduce the dosage. We want you to be able to live a normal life and do what you want to do. But the night you partied did happen. I don't think there's much to gain by lowering your medication, and I think if we do, there's an elevated risk of a potential seizure breakthrough. But altogether, it feels like things are going well. Do you have any other questions or concerns?"

"There is one other thing. Next year I'm going to climb to the top of Mount Kilimanjaro. I'm hearing the altitude up there is no joke. Do you think that could be an issue?"

I could tell he wasn't expecting that one.

"Oh . . . okay," he said. "Well. As far as I know, nobody has taken a randomized group of people with epilepsy to climb Mount Kilimanjaro, so I'm not sure we have much data on this. Generally speaking, what I say is if you're seizure free and you're doing well, you can do a lot of things with a few exceptions. Like, don't ever scuba dive. Having a seizure while you're deep underwater like that would be extremely dangerous. Certain things like that are bad ideas."

Damn. Scratch that one off the bucket list. I always wanted to go scuba diving.

"Don't ever go skydiving either. You have to think to yourself, 'What would happen if I had a seizure while doing this activity? Am I somewhere that people can take care of me or would it be a problem?'"

"Right."

No skydiving either? I didn't like the direction this conversation was going. Good thing Renee wasn't around to hear this. I may need to get a second opinion.

"As far as Kilimanjaro . . . We know that people who have epilepsy are at a higher risk of having sleep apnea, which is when your throat closes up at night and you don't get as much oxygen. We know that those people's seizures can get worse. So it's possible that if you're at altitude and not getting as much oxygen, that could provoke a seizure. Honestly, I do think there's probably an increased risk of that happening up there. But there are also lots of risks we take everyday, right? Part of life is deciding what your risk tolerance is."

"It's possible I could have a seizure while I'm driving, but I still own over two hundred cars and drive them daily," I pointed out.

"There you go. What I'll say is, if you are dead set on doing this, you should prepare knowing that a seizure could happen so that there is a plan in place in the event that one does."

"Most definitely. That's what I'll do."

I thanked the doctor for his time and headed out to the parking lot. On my drive home, I tried to think of ways I could sugarcoat what he said. It wasn't a flat-out "no" but it most definitely wasn't the "all clear" I'd been hoping for. I knew it wouldn't be enough to put my sister's concerns to rest.

Then I thought about those blue and pink pills that would be waiting for me on my nightstand when I got home. There was a part of my mind telling me this was all a conspiracy to control a wealthy black man and keep me from climbing Mount Kilimanjaro and realizing my full potential. It's like as soon as I made some money, they tried to control me psychologically and get me addicted to medications to limit my greatness. Who *really* decided that these pills were what's best for me?

Whoever it was, I wanted to tell them to shove all those pills up their ass.

CHAPTER

8

THE BOX

I'D THOUGHT THE BIGGEST THING I'D HAVE to worry about on Kilimanjaro would have been a monkey attack, but it turns out those are extremely rare. The most serious threat on the climb would be the altitude, and in my case, the potential for my preexisting medical conditions to worsen at those altitudes.

Seizures were not the only thing I had to consider.

Despite my recent weight loss, I was still technically considered obese. That could play a factor. *How many handsome obese niggas had made it to the top of Mount Kilimanjaro?* I wondered. I may need an entire team of medical professionals to assess my situation. My hope was at least one of them would give me the green light.

These were questions for my primary care physician. I would also have to consult my orthopedic surgeon. I was two years removed from having a hip replacement. How would my new hip hold up throughout this climb? Would I feel that cold titanium inside my body as I ascended the mountain and the temperature dropped?

Then there was the weed issue. This one was a double whammy. Not only did I need to consult with a physician about my smoking habits, but I would also have to speak with my attorney. I found out Tanzania is incredibly strict when it comes to drugs, weed included. I'd already had a few homies get detained in foreign countries for having a couple of joints in their carry-on.

I smoke pretty much from the moment I wake up in the morning until I call it a night. Is it the healthiest habit? Probably not. I'm just trying to keep it real with you guys. Inhaling smoke while I was at altitude—where I was already at a higher risk of having a seizure—sounded like a recipe for disaster.

Could I just cut down on it, or would I have to stop smoking altogether? If so, would I quit cold-turkey right before the trip, or should I gradually taper off in the months leading up to the climb? What about edibles or tinctures? I didn't care for those. Edibles and hiking? Nah. There had to be a better solution. What if I stopped smoking my beloved grape Swisher Sweets and substituted organic hemp rolling papers? I think I could do that. Would it make a difference?

This was a complex problem. And complex problems require creative solutions. Any respectable doctor would just tell me to lay off the weed, but I knew if I did that I'd be miserable the whole trip. There had to be another option.

I decided to seek counsel outside of the medical industrial complex. I've got a homegirl who's deep into the health and wellness communities. She's into some real out-there, hippie shit. The last time we spoke she had just received a shipment of live bees to her crib. She had acquired these bees with the intention of stinging herself with them. According to her, bee venom contains medicinal properties. I don't give a fuck what condition I end up with. You're not going to see Rozay stinging himself with bees. Some things are just too much.

But I do find some of the shit she's into interesting, and I appreciate her outside-the-box perspective. I reached out and told her my plan and my concerns with regard to the altitude. To my surprise, her recommendation wasn't to go outside the box. It was to go *inside* a box. That's how I got put on to the hypobaric chamber.

A hypobaric chamber is not the same thing as a hyp*er*baric chamber. Prior to this conversation, I wasn't familiar with either of them. The only chamber I knew about was the one a bullet goes into. That's neither here nor there.

Hyp*er*baric chambers were first developed in the 1600s and are still used today to treat a number of medical conditions. It's a sealed, pressurized tube where a patient inhales pure oxygen under increased pressure. The added pressure helps the body absorb more oxygen. It can be used as a lifesaving treatment in extreme cases, like if someone gets carbon monoxide poisoning in their house or decompression sickness from scuba diving. You also see elite athletes use hyperbaric chambers to reduce inflammation and speed up their recovery from injury, including the likes of LeBron James, Michael Phelps, Usain Bolt, and Terrell Owens.

As you heard, I was recently banned from scuba diving for life, so I was not in the market for a hyperbaric chamber. I would be entering a hyp*o*baric chamber, which is not a tube, but a glass box. It's a room—and it's not a normal room. Hypobaric chambers are specialized sealed environments where air pressure can be lowered to simulate high-altitude conditions. By reducing atmospheric pressure and oxygen levels inside the chamber, it re-creates the feeling of being at higher elevation. The use of hypobaric chambers started as a way to train military pilots and astronauts and test how their bodies would react to certain environments. Mountain climbers use them to pre-acclimatize their bodies before attempting to climb places like Mount Everest.

Or places like Kilimanjaro.

The box contained three things: a chair, a treadmill, and a stationary bicycle. Given that this was my first session, I was advised by the facility's staff to stick with the chair. They attached a fingertip monitor to measure my heart rate and blood oxygen saturation, which would measure the percentage of hemoglobin in my red blood cells saturated with oxygen. Then I was given an oxygen mask that I could put on if I started to feel like I was going to pass out.

The box was sealed, and they started to bring me up in elevation. The first thing I felt was my fingers tingling. I remembered the shrooms fiasco. *Not this shit again.*

My breathing became more labored. But then some wild shit happened. As the altitude increased and the pressure dropped, it got colder and the air inside the room changed. There was actual fog and mist in the chamber, just like there would be on the mountain.

After the first minute or two—I can't remember—I reached for my clipboard to complete the exercise they'd assigned me before I went in: write down my full name and date of birth. Too easy, I thought. I started but after a few seconds I just stopped. My mind had gone blank. I was frozen. I looked down at the paper and it just said:

WIL—

I quickly took a hit of the oxygen mask. Immediately, I regained all my senses. The room gradually warmed up and the mist dissipated. They'd brought the box back down to normal. *Damn.* I thought I had been doing pretty well up there. I felt alright now. If anything, just a little foggy. But that altitude had come out of nowhere and turned Rozay into a statue.

I wasn't sure what to make of my hypobaric chamber experience. On my drive home, I called up a mountaineer friend of mine to get a second opinion.

"Look, it's interesting technology," he said. "But that shit costs a lot of money for something that's not a guarantee. My opinion is it's not worth it. The way to train for this is for you to get in the best shape possible. Are you working with a personal trainer and a nutritionist? As far as the altitude, I think you just have to be there on the mountain for as long as possible beforehand to let your body naturally acclimate. That's the only way you're going to succeed."

Deep down, I knew he was right. Under the pretense of "thinking outside the box," I was really looking for an easy way out of the preparation and hard work it would require for me to actually pull this climb off.

The truth is, before you can think outside the box, you have to start inside the box. The box is your domain. It's where you need to be proficient and put in your ten thousand hours of practice before you start looking outside it. The box contains crucial information. It stores history, techniques, and best practices. It's where you find the fundamentals. I'm a master of my craft when it comes to music, but when it came to mountaineering, I was a novice.

The idea of thinking outside the box is another example of the paradoxes found within the creative process. Thinking or doing something new just for the sake of it usually results in lame shit. The most interesting rulebreakers are the ones who deeply understand and respect the rules—then decide to push those boundaries. My guy Pablo Picasso mastered classical realism before he invented Cubism and blew everyone's domes.

I had gone into a box claiming I was thinking outside the box, but in reality I was just avoiding the most important box.

That sounds a little confusing, so let me simplify it. That hypobaric chamber was me trying to skip steps and cut corners. I had to be honest with myself. I wasn't going about this climb the right way. If I really wanted to do this shit, I had to fully commit to the process and everything it entailed.

And if I didn't really want to do it, then I had to keep it moving and figure out something else.

CHAPTER 9

FROM MANIFESTATION TO PROCRASTINATION

BEFORE I HAD LOOKED INTO ANY DETAILS or considered the logistics of climbing Mount Kilimanjaro, I revealed my plan to the world. This was shortly after I'd had my initial epiphany. I first made the announcement while I was being interviewed for some podcast I had scheduled that week.

"This is the first time I'm saying this . . . I've given myself a challenge. Next year, I'm going to hike to the top of Mount Kilimanjaro."

"Wow. Where is that?"

"Africa."

"And what's the challenge?"

"Just to make it to the top."

"How does one go about doing this? Have you looked into it?"

"I don't look into nothing. I make up my mind and then I get it done. I said next year, so for the rest of this year I'm preparing myself mentally. Then next year I'll start getting ready physically."

"How long does it take to get to the top?

"Who knows."

"And what's the elevation up there?"

"I'm not sure."

"Are you going by yourself?"

"Of course not. Somebody will have to be there to carry the Wingstop."

> Rick Ross Announces Plan to Climb Mount Kilimanjaro
>
> *Mediaite*

> Rick Ross Explains His Plan To Climb Mount Kilimanjaro
>
> *HotNewHipHop*

> Rick Ross Says He Wants to Climb Mount Kilimanjaro
>
> *Rap-Up*

My announcement got picked up by the blogs. That was by design. Speaking my dreams into existence has always been my modus operandi. Remember, I was dead broke when I started calling myself the biggest boss. That was at a time when I still had to borrow money from my momma to keep my car from getting repossessed, and I was out here claiming to be the biggest boss. Nobody took me or my dreams seriously back then. Why would they? They sounded far-fetched.

But ambitious goals, like love or spiritual pursuits, can often seem to contradict logic.

I'm a big believer in the power of manifestation and the law of attraction—that positive thoughts and beliefs shape your reality. It's taken me far in life. Saying your goals out loud reinforces your belief in those goals, and belief drives behavior. You're more likely to take action and follow through on your goals when you speak and hear them out loud.

The other reason I announced my idea was that it would serve as a bat-signal. My hope was that it would lead to new connections and resources. I wanted to get in touch with the best high-altitude mountain-hiking trainer. I wanted recommendations for the best tour guide companies in Tanzania. I wanted to secure a brand partnership with REI or Patagonia to sponsor the trip and lace me with the best gear. When you put your vision out into the world, people see it. We'll get into the power of creative collaboration later.

Based on my answers to the interviewer's basic questions about climbing Mount Kilimanjaro, it's obvious I didn't know what the fuck I was talking about. When you're just beginning to brainstorm ideas, I think that's fine. There will eventually come a time when you have to get practical and start looking at things with a sober analysis. But when I made my declaration on that podcast, I hadn't yet reached that stage of the creative process. I was still in the first stage. And that's when you're allowed to dream big without placing any limits or filters on it. Let your mind roam freely and imagine possibilities that sound impossible.

You don't need to have everything figured out from the jump. The limits and constraints will show up in due time. Try to have a little fun before they do.

From there, you'll start to gather information. You'll throw paint on the wall and see what sticks. Let your ideas develop naturally and see where they take you.

I also thought that if I went public with my plan, it would motivate me to follow through. Making the external commitment would hold me accountable and push me to do whatever was required to bring this crazy idea to fruition. This approach had worked for me countless times in the past.

Unfortunately, that's not how things played out. I'm not sure what I meant when I told the interviewer I would be spending the rest of the year preparing myself mentally. But ultimately, what ended up happening was I lost momentum. My inner circle wasn't on board with the idea. The medical professionals had expressed some of their concerns. The hypobaric chamber was cool but halfway through I was unable to write my name. There was a series of setbacks that resulted in the climb falling by the wayside. I became distracted by other things and never ended up hiring a personal trainer or nutritionist.

The final nail in the coffin came from Lupe Fiasco. Fifteen years earlier, on January 12, 2010, Lupe Fiasco successfully reached the Uhuru Peak of Mount Kilimanjaro. He'd done the climb alongside a group of famous celebrities—Jessica Biel, Emile Hirsch, Kenna, and Santigold—as part of an initiative to raise awareness and money for the global clean water crisis.

Initially, I wasn't aware of this. If I had been, I would've hit Lupe from the jump and gotten the inside scoop. Lupe and I aren't close, but we have done a few records together over the years and I trust his opinion. Anyone familiar with Lupe's music knows he's an extremely intelligent individual. But like I said, I didn't know that he had done the climb.

Evee, my GM at Maybach Music Group, however, was aware of this. And once she found out about my crazy idea, she started reaching out to people until she was able to get Lupe on a call with my sister. Apparently, when Renee told Lupe about my intentions, he sounded skeptical.

"To this day, that was the hardest thing I've ever done," he told her. "Keep in mind, this was fifteen years ago. I was twenty-seven years old. How old is your brother now?"

"Forty-nine."

"Yeah, I don't know . . ."

Renee had heard enough. After her conversation with Lupe, she called me and told me the trip wasn't happening. My health was too important.

As much as I value my big sister's input, of course, I'm still the biggest boss. I make my own decisions. I told her I'd sleep on it and let her know my final decision in the morning.

Later that evening, I tried to find the documentary that MTV had produced on Lupe's climb, but it wasn't available to watch online. I was able to find some clips from it, and I also watched an interview Jessica, Kenna, and Emile did with Larry King on CNN, where they discussed their experience.

"At one point I went to our medic and asked her why I had a headache that was completely surrounding my head," Kenna told Larry. "And she said it was because my brain was swelling into my head cavity. That didn't make me happy. It made me feel like I was doing something crazy."

My brain swelling into my head cavity? The reality that climbing Mount Kilimanjaro was a bad idea for me was becoming more evident with every new piece of information I took in. I could no longer ignore what my sister, my doctors, Evee, and Lupe were trying to tell me.

I called my sister in the morning and told her the trip was off. I would have to figure out another idea for the book.

Manifestation without action is nothing more than wishful thinking. If saying your goal out loud is all you've got, it won't be long before that genius idea fizzles out and vanishes into the ether. I encourage everyone to dream big, but to actually bring a dream to life requires planning, preparation, and execution.

What I learned from this process is that every big idea is made up of a series of smaller ideas. Those smaller ideas are often less sexy and exciting than that initial creative spark. To bring a vision to fruition requires planning, preparation, and follow through. I never reached that stage of the process.

When the idea to climb Mount Kilimanjaro first came to me, it was a vision of the end result. Of me standing at the summit planting my flag. I wasn't thinking about altitude sickness. I wasn't thinking about my health risks. And, on a smaller level, I wasn't thinking about other details, like not being able to shower for over a week. I wasn't thinking about eating porridge every meal and then having to shit it out into a hole in the ground later. The more I learned about those things, the more I started to fold on the whole idea.

An ambitious creative endeavor can be long, messy, and at times uncertain. There will be setbacks and uncomfortable moments along the way. If you get into something just for the end result, it usually won't be worth it.

There are beginning, middle, and late stages to the creative process, but most of your time will be spent in the thick of the middle part, after the initial excitement wears off and before the rewards of the finish line come into sight. If you come to the realization that you can't find joy and fulfillment in the harder parts of the process, it's probably best to move on before you burn out. There's no shame in doing that.

Any artist who has achieved any measure of success will tell you that in the shadow of every great creation, there are a dozen discarded drafts and failed attempts. Failure is a part of the creative process.

CHAPTER

10

A CHANGE IN PLANS

MONTHS PASSED AND I WAS STILL IN SEARCH of something that would reignite my creative spirit. I also needed to figure out the book. The publisher had sent a couple emails asking for an update. I hadn't gotten back to them, but I couldn't put them off for much longer. I knew I still wanted to break out of my regularly scheduled programming and *do* something I'd never done before. I just hadn't figured out what that was quite yet.

Then one day, it came to me. I was at home and decided to put on Netflix to find something to watch. There had to be some true crime docuseries on there I hadn't seen yet. Some gruesome murder committed against a spouse for a life insurance payout. It's a tale as old as time—or at least as long as life insurance payouts have existed.

As soon as the Netflix homepage loaded, I saw a preview on the screen with something familiar—something that belonged to me: a vintage wood-paneled Jeep Grand Wagoneer. Upon closer inspection, I realized it wasn't actually mine. This particular Woody was a darker blue. There were two people in the car: I didn't recognize the driver, but the person riding shotgun had an instantly recognizable face. It was Will Ferrell.

What I was seeing was a trailer for Will Ferrell's

upcoming documentary, where he and his friend had embarked on a cross-country road trip from New York City to the Santa Monica pier in Los Angeles.

Just like that, lightning had struck once again. A road trip.

I could take a cross-country road trip.

Would I be ripping off Will Ferrell? Hell nah. His documentary wasn't even out yet, so I had no idea where he'd gone and I doubted there would be much, if any, overlap. For starters, I wouldn't be leaving from New York. The Rozay Road Trip would begin at the Promise Land in Fayetteville, Georgia.

If I was biting *Will & Harper*, that meant Will was biting *Thelma & Louise*, which was biting *Easy Rider*, which would be a rip-off of Jack Kerouac's 1957 novel *On the Road*. I could keep going, but we already covered how there's no such thing as a truly original idea. The cross-country road trip is a time-honored tradition, one that's commonly associated with themes of exploration, adventure, and self-discovery. This was similar in premise to what I had wanted to achieve with the Kilimanjaro idea, but this shit was more up my alley. I could tailor the trip so our stops aligned with my hobbies and interests.

Now, don't get me wrong, I travel all the time. On average, I'm probably in three different cities every week. But nine times out of ten, when I go somewhere, I see three locations: the airport, the concert venue, and the hotel I'm staying in. The vast majority of my travels have been business-related, so I don't get to do a lot of sightseeing.

The only thing that would qualify as me swagger jacking would be if I took my Grand Wagoneer. Will Ferrell had beaten me to that one. I had to give it to him: he'd picked the perfect iconic car to evoke the image of the great American road trip.

So then which one of my cars would I take? The good news was I had options—and two hundred of those options were right here at the Promise Land.

I closed my eyes and started running through my car collection. I visualized different combinations of cars and various national landmarks. My Ferrari F8 Spider at the Grand Canyon. My military-grade Humvee with the custom Louis Vuitton leather seats at Rocky Mountain National Park. My Cybertruck in Roswell, New Mexico. That would be a good vehicle to let the extraterrestrials know Rozay comes in peace.

Any of those images would make for an iconic book cover. But each option had its drawbacks. As fun as my Ferrari is to drive, it probably wasn't the most comfortable choice for an extended road trip. And I'd only be able to bring one other person with me. The Humvee would be able to withstand any adversity I might encounter along the way, but it was lacking when it came to its sound system and in-car entertainment. And if I took the Cybertruck, that meant that every three hundred miles, I'd need to take an hour-long break at an electric vehicle charging station.

I thought about Mount Kilimanjaro and how I'd bitten off more than I could chew. I didn't want to make similar mistakes this time around. I needed to make a practical choice. The more I considered it, the more I started thinking maybe I didn't want to have to do all that driving. What if I got a driver? That would free me up to fully take in the sights of the open road and have some thought-provoking conversations with my crew.

What if I got a tour bus? That way I could bring along whoever I wanted and we wouldn't have to be crammed in there like sardines. I'd have room to spread out. I'd have a bathroom on board so we could cut down on rest stops, where I'd inevitably encounter fans. One of the reasons I haven't done a lot of recreational traveling is because being famous can take some of the fun out of being a tourist. There's nothing worse than a motherfucker trying to take a selfie with you in a public restroom. Have some self-respect and let Rozay urinate in peace. Another pro of a bus.

It had been a long time since I'd chartered a tour bus. These days I had my jet, and before that I flew commercial. The thought of being on a bus again brought me back to the beginning of my career. The whirlwind year of 2006 right after "Hustlin'" dropped. When I was hitting a new city every night, performing the record that had changed my life. That was such an exciting time for me. I wanted to feel that energy again.

I called Renee.

"Let the publisher know I'm taking a cross-country road trip. Let's pull up the calendar, figure out a date, and then I'm going to need you to book a tour bus . . ."

"Okay, Will," she said. "That all sounds fine to me."

As far as my sister was concerned, a cross-country road trip was a big improvement from me attempting to climb Mount Kilimanjaro. It was safer, cheaper, and easier to pull off. But when she informed the people at the publisher of my new plan, they didn't start doing cartwheels. Their response was lukewarm at best.

CHAPTER
11

ART, COMMERCE, AND THE SEPARATION OF CHURCH AND STATE

THE PUBLISHER HAD FOUND OUT ABOUT MY Kilimanjaro idea via my podcast announcement. They hadn't loved that idea either. For one thing, they were well aware—probably more than I was at the time—that an undertaking like that would require a great deal of planning and preparation. That meant they would likely have to grant me an extension of the manuscript delivery date. And *that* would result in them having to push back the book's publication date, which meant it would take longer for them to recoup the advance they'd paid out.

But that wasn't even their biggest issue. Their main concern seemed to be that my goal of becoming a mountaineer wasn't in line with their original concept for a book about creativity. And they felt the same way about this latest road trip iteration of the book.

"We thought the goal was to model the book a bit like *Creative Quest* by Questlove."

This was not the first time we had run into this issue. A few months following the release of my debut, *Hurricanes*, I re-upped with them to do a second book. It was pitched as a self-help/business book, which I thought was a dope idea. My memoir had been the story of my life up to that point. It had only scratched the surface as far as my business ventures went. I was looking forward to diving deeper into that part of me in my second book. But by the time I got around to start writing it, the world had changed.

It was the Spring of 2020 and the COVID-19 pandemic was in full effect. Like for many people, it upended my whole way of life. I went from being on the road every weekend to being stuck at home under quarantine. At the time, show money was still my most lucrative stream of revenue. That had disappeared overnight, and there was no telling if or when things would ever get back to normal. So I had to make adjustments and find new ways to sustain and continue growing my empire. As it turns out, living under lockdown made for a good time to focus on writing a book. As I began working on it, I couldn't help but talk about the unprecedented moment I was living in and the underlying business philosophies behind the moves I was making at the time. But when the publisher saw an early outline of *The Perfect Day to Boss Up*, they became concerned that I'd veered off track. They thought there was too much focus on COVID-19 and voiced hesitation about the approach and sensibility of the book. "This outline doesn't reflect the project we commissioned," they said. "We had discussed a prescriptive business book."

The publisher wanted us to go back to the drawing board and come up with a new outline.

This was followed by a second email suggesting I look at books like *The Gucci Mane Guide to Greatness* and *The 50th Law* by 50 Cent as examples. I couldn't believe these people would even mention Woodface to me. You've got to know how to talk to Rozay.

A younger me would have gone bad on them, but instead I got back to work on the book that I wanted to write. How did that turn out? *The Perfect Day to Boss Up* debuted at number five on the *New York Times* bestseller list and would remain on the list for months. It sold even better than my first book.

I knew this song and dance all too well. I was still a relative newcomer to the world of book publishing, but this wasn't Rozay's first rodeo. I come from the music industry. Do you know how many times some record label executive or A&R rep has tried to tell me I need a feature from some flash-in-the-pan artist in order for my next album to sell? Or that I need to get beats from the hot producer of the moment? I had to sit through many of those types of conversations early on in my career. Thankfully, after twenty years in the rap game, I've reached a point where most of the suits know better than to try to interfere with my music.

Model my book after Questlove's? Don't get it twisted. I'm a fan of Questlove. As a matter of fact, I've gotten to perform with Questlove on multiple occasions. Every time I ever got booked to perform on *The Tonight Show Starring Jimmy Fallon*, I was honored to hit the stage with a drummer as talented as Quest and a band as legendary as the Roots.

In fact, I've been *inspired* and *influenced* by working with Questlove. Those *Tonight Show* performances were some of my first experiences getting to rehearse and perform my music alongside a live band. Those shows planted seeds in my mind. Seeds that would eventually grow and lead to me doing things like NPR's *Tiny Desk*, or Red Bull Symphonic, a concert where I was backed by an all-black orchestra at Atlanta Symphony Hall.

As a businessman, I could appreciate the publisher's position. Their feedback was a reflection of their business model. A business's goal is to generate profits. In order to keep generating profits on a consistent basis, a good business has to identify and manage their risk. After all, people's jobs and livelihoods are at stake if a company goes belly up. The result of this is risk-averse decision-making.

One of the most reliable ways to minimize risk is to do something that already has a proven track record of success. If it doesn't work and you get called into your boss's office, at least you'll have an explanation when they ask you what the fuck you were thinking. But let me not speak too much against my own self-interest or I may not get to release a fourth book.

Anyway, the problem is that the blueprint then becomes "people who liked *this* will also like *this*." You see this type of thinking across all types of industries, especially entertainment. Predictability sells. Franchises, sequels, reboots, and remakes have a built-in customer base.

Like I said, as a businessman, I get it. I purchased my first Wingstop franchise in 2011. When it did well, I didn't follow that up by opening up a molecular gastronomy restaurant with a prix fixe tasting menu. I went the DJ Khaled route and bought another one. And then another one. And then another one. Eventually I got up to over thirty locations. But fast-food franchising is a business venture of mine. It is not one of my creative pursuits.

The good people at my book publisher have been great business partners. But we are not creative partners. Creativity and risk management do not go together. Artistic work is not about playing things safe, making people happy, or ensuring that everyone keeps their jobs. Art is about taking risks and pushing the envelope. As a creator, I believe artists have a responsibility to hold the line between church and state. Otherwise, there's a good chance the wrong motherfuckers are going to insert themselves into your idea, and they may very well dilute your product.

In *The War of Art*, author Steven Pressfield explores the psychology of creativity. In a chapter titled "The Definition of a Hack," Pressfield calls out so-called artists who approach their work not from a place of genuine inspiration, but out of a desire for a certain result from it, whether it be monetary gain or the approval and acceptance of others.

"The hack writes hierarchically. He writes what he imagines will play well in the eyes of others. He does not ask himself, What do I myself want to write? . . . Instead he asks, What's hot, what can I make a deal for?"

Pressfield's first book was the 1995 novel *The Legend of Bagger Vance*. That book went on to be a bestseller. Not only that, Dreamworks Pictures and 20th Century Fox acquired the movie rights and turned it into a major motion picture starring Matt Damon and my guy Will Smith.

But Pressfield didn't write *The Legend of Bagger Vance* because he thought Will Smith would be champing at the bit to play Bagger on the big screen. At the time he wrote it, something like that probably seemed implausible.

Pressfield was pretty sure nobody else would see his vision. But that didn't matter to him. Because it was *his* vision. There was a story in his mind that he needed to put down on paper. I know that feeling. Those are the types of instincts that result in original work instead of safe, mid-tier shit that takes no creative risk.

As an artist, I am influenced and inspired by many different sources. But I don't go and model my anything after anybody, and I most definitely don't compromise my creative vision. I set trends. I don't follow them. My book, whatever it ended up being, would be something that felt true and authentic to me.

But the publisher had nothing to worry about. It's not like I was planning to do these people like I was André 3000 when he came back from a seventeen-year hiatus with an album of him playing the flute for ninety minutes. This is Rozay we're talking about. I always hit the sweet spot where art and commerce get to coexist. I write hit records and I write bestselling books. I'm the Blockbuster Boss, baby!

I came up with a compromise that I felt would satisfy all parties. The road trip would carry on as planned, but I would pick up a copy of Questlove's book and see if it sparked any ideas for my book. It was a gesture of good faith to show the publisher that I appreciated their feedback.

And guess what? *The Creative Quest* is a dope read. Shout-out to Questlove. I most definitely picked up some game from reading his book. I even have a favorite passage from it, and it just so happens to be about the topic we're covering right now. It's on page 216.

"Who gets to determine when an artist is on track and when an artist is off track? The artist is the track."

"So how do you want me to respond to the email?" my sister asked.

"Just tell them we already paid for the bus."

CHAPTER

12

STAY CHILDISH

I SCHEDULED THE ROAD TRIP FOR THE WEEK of November 4, 2024. The only thing I had on my calendar that week was my Las Vegas residency at Drai's on the ninth. So we had to get to Vegas by Saturday. That was the only nonnegotiable.

When it comes to creativity, things like deadlines, final deliverables, and budgets can feel like constraints. Factors that limit creative potential more than they fuel it. That's not necessarily true. One of the reasons my Mount Kilimanjaro idea fizzled out was that I never actually set a firm date for the climb. I never booked flights or put down a deposit with a travel company. Without a timetable or deadline in place, it was easy for me to put off finding a trainer or nutritionist to get in shape. Deadlines inject a sense of urgency into the creative process. Urgency creates pressure. And pressure makes diamonds.

I've always worked well under pressure. Some of my best music has come at the eleventh hour. On Wednesday, May 26, 2010, I recorded a song called "B.M.F." If you're familiar with my catalog, you know the song. "B.M.F." was the biggest hit off my fourth album, *Teflon Don*, which dropped July 20, 2010. What you may not know is that I didn't record "B.M.F." for *Teflon Don*.

May 26, 2010, was the Wednesday heading into Memorial Day Weekend. I was getting ready to drop *The Albert Anastasia EP* the next day. I wanted to put out a mixtape before the holiday weekend to set the tone for the summer and build momentum leading up to my album release in July. "B.M.F" was recorded just hours before *Albert Anastasia* hit the internet. The response to it (and "MC Hammer") was so big I had to add it to *Teflon Don* when it dropped two months later. It clearly worked out for the best.

Setting a date for the road trip and having that "be in Vegas by Saturday" deadline gave me just enough structure to start drawing up a loose plan. I didn't need an hour-by-hour daily itinerary. I wanted to line up a couple cool spots to visit but also leave room for unexpected twists and turns. I was aiming to find the balance of another paradox within the creative process: the need for structure versus the need for freedom.

I had wanted to hit the road first thing Monday morning, but I ended up having to push our departure to Tuesday. The week before, I got a last-minute booking request for a show in Dubai on November 3, and the United Arab Emirates made an offer I couldn't refuse. I didn't get back to Atlanta until Monday afternoon. As I unpacked my suitcase from my quick trip overseas and started to pack for the road trip ahead, I was feeling exhausted.

Tuesday, November 5, was Election Day. I would be traveling across the country as Americans decided if they were ready for the first black female president or if they wanted to bring Donald Trump back for another four years. I don't want to get too into politics, but that was an added element to the trip. It was by design. My thinking was that, in the event I didn't have any meaningful creative insights or awakenings, at least I might have a civil war I could talk about.

I had a small crew with me. I had Neil mapping out the trip and lining up spots for us to check out. I also invited my masseuse Joanne to help me recover from my quick turnaround trip to Dubai and the physical strain I knew was coming in the week ahead from sitting on the bus for hours on end. I had security with me too—Jerry and Taz—just in case the aforementioned civil war broke out. Last but not least, I was planning on bringing two of my day-one homies—Kano and Slab—along for their company and comic relief.

Unfortunately, both Kano and Slab had to drop out at the last minute. Kano was managing Nino Breeze, my newest addition to the MMG roster. Nino's single "Type A Nigga," was starting to take off, and he was getting requests for shows and interviews left and right. I made the executive decision for Kano to stay back and handle business on behalf of the team.

Slab had his bag packed and was ready to go when he received the tragic news that his mother had passed away. I felt terrible for my brother. Slab is a one-of-one individual. His presence on the trip would be missed. But there was nothing to say other than to tell him I loved him and that I'd see him when I got back.

The road trip was already off to a rocky start, and we hadn't even exited the gates of the Promise Land. But the show had to go on. I had a book to write and a creative rut to bust out of.

Our driver for the week was a middle-aged white guy by the name of Buddy Ramsey. Buddy shared a last name similar to that of the British celebrity chef Gordon Ramsay, but he actually resembled another famous restaurateur: Guy Fieri. Buddy was Guy Fieri's doppelganger. Or maybe he was his evil twin. I didn't know Buddy, but my first impression was that he seemed like a good guy.

Buddy was the owner of the coach rental service company. His days of actually driving tour buses across the country were in the rearview. But when he got word that the biggest boss was chartering his Prevost XLII "Soprano" bus for the week, he decided to get back behind the wheel for one more go.

I boarded the bus and took inventory of the accommodations. A lounge area with a forty-seven-inch TV. A kitchenette with a fridge, microwave, and Keurig machine. A bathroom with a shower. Twelve bunkbeds. The basics. I wasn't planning on sleeping on the bus, so this would be sufficient.

I made my way toward the back, where there was a second lounge. This would be my spot for the week. I connected my phone to the sound system to test out the acoustics and then cut on the TV to see what onboard entertainment options there would be. The bus was equipped with high-speed internet, so I'd have Netflix, Hulu, Amazon Prime, Apple TV, and YouTube at my fingertips.

Buddy came to the back to let me know our bags were loaded and we were ready to go. And with that, we were off.

Two and a half hours into the journey, we arrived at our first stop: the Barber Vintage Motorsports Museum in Birmingham, Alabama. The Barber Museum is recognized by the Guiness Book of World Records as having the world's largest motorcycle collection, as well as the world's largest collection of Lotus race cars. I had heard about the museum for years but had never found the time to make the trip out to Birmingham to see it with my own eyes. I was looking forward to it. This place was my Disneyland.

From the moment I stepped inside the Barber Museum, I was in awe. That shit was stunning. I'm not even talking about the motorcycles or the whips. I'll get to those in a minute. First I have to tell you about the architecture of the building.

The museum is a two-hundred-and-thirty-thousand-square-foot, multi-level structure of concrete, steel, and glass. I'm talking an ultra-modern, open-concept design. Floor-to-ceiling glass walls look out on the 2.38-mile racetrack that's behind the museum. When we first pulled up, I couldn't see just how much more there was to the place. It turned out the museum is just one part of the larger Barber

Motorsports Park, a racing facility that spans 880 acres and hosts the IndyCar Series's Grand Prix of Alabama every year. As I toured the museum, I could hear the constant roar of superbikes and race cars circling the track outside.

In the middle of the museum there's a huge glass-walled freight elevator. With the push of a button, I started to ascend. Passing me by were panoramic views of all five floors of car and motorcycle displays. My eyes darted in every direction. There were just so many things to marvel at—thousands of gorgeous motor vehicles vying for my attention.

They probably had a hundred Harley-Davidsons alone, representing every era, all the way back to the early 1900s. Rare midcentury British classics hung suspended in midair, dangling from the ceiling like monkeys in *The Planet of the Apes*. There were these shelf-like steel towers, with each level featuring bright and bold Japanese superbikes—Hondas, Yamahas, Kawasakis, and Suzukis. They had everything. It was overwhelming.

If you're wondering if the good people at the Barber Museum rolled out the red carpet for Rozay and gave me the VIP treatment, the answer is yes, of course they did. I've got to give a shout-out to my man Robert for taking care of us that day. After touring all of the museum's five floors, Robert brought us downstairs to an area that's not open to the public: the restoration shop.

This was where the magic happened. This was where the museum's team of expert technicians worked on restoring vintage motorcycles and cars. One of the dopest things about this museum is that the vast majority of the bikes on display have been restored to running condition. You could take almost any of them and ride it right off its display ramp, out the garage, and onto the Barber racetrack for a spin. These folks were not just preserving history. They were keeping that history alive.

I felt like a kid in a candy shop. There were so many options I didn't know where to look. After regaining my composure, I decided to approach this place the way I'd viewed the Estefans' Picasso painting. At first I stood back and took everything in. Then I narrowed my focus to certain exhibits. Then to individual motorcycles. Then to the engines and other individual parts.

I've learned over time that when you take things in from different physical vantage points to shift your mental perspective, you come away with different observations. I always try to view something through multiple lenses or listen to something through multiple filters because it ultimately makes for a deeper and richer understanding of whatever it is you're trying to absorb.

It was down there in the body shop, surveying everything from different vantage points, that something caught my eye. It was one of the smallest items in the museum, but it blew my dome back with more force than anything else I saw that day. And this was a place full of mind-blowing items.

Sitting on top of a wooden workbench was a green-and-yellow remote-controlled car. It was a 1:3 scale model of a Lotus 49 Formula One racing car. Sitting inside it was a figurine of British racing driver Jim Clark, who won the 1967 Dutch Grand Prix in that very car.

I knew there was something different about it, but I couldn't put my finger on what it was. As I got closer, I could tell it wasn't made of plastic like most remote-controlled cars. I reached out to touch it and confirmed my suspicion: aluminum. I tried to lift it, but it barely budged. It must have weighed over sixty pounds.

"You like that?" Robert asked. "That right there is a running car."

"What do you mean?" I asked.

"It has a V-8 engine, just like the original engine used in the full-size Lotus 49."

"That's not possible."

"It is. There's a niche, specialized manufacturer that builds these miniature-scale engines with amazing precision. It has all the working parts just like a full-size engine:

pistons, valves, eight carburetors—the whole deal. You can start it and rev it just like its big brother."

"And the rest?"

"This guy—he's from the Netherlands—he got a hold of one of these mini engines and then he built this replica—every single part of it—to scale."

This was not a toy. This was a masterpiece in miniature engineering. This was designed and assembled by hand to replicate the exact proportions, materials, and details of the original Lotus 49. These were all real automotive components: miniature working disc brakes, mini suspension, mini custom tires, everything. This was the equivalent result to if Rick Moranis had put an actual Lotus 49 in his *Honey, I Shrunk the Kids* machine.

I needed to find this Dutch gentleman and shake his hand. This man was a hobbyist, he was an artist, and he

was a NASA-level engineer. The definition of a master craftsman. The level of precise detail and aesthetic accuracy was unbelievable. It was fucking me up! It must have taken a thousand hours to build this. I didn't even want to think about what it cost to make it or how much the Barber Museum had paid to acquire it. There wasn't a high enough price. Something like this was truly priceless.

I realize that for some people, my collection of more than two hundred cars might come across as some over-the-top rich nigga shit. I get it. I can see why someone would view it that way, and on some level it's true. But I don't collect these cars just to stunt. I do it because cars are something that I'm truly passionate about. They've brought me joy for as long as I can remember.

When I saw that remote-controlled Lotus, I remembered the feeling of playing with my own RC cars when I was just a jit. I remembered how excited I was when I got my first Grasshopper two-wheel-drive off-road buggy. Tamiya released that kit in 1984, when I was eight years old. It was the cheapest RC car they offered at the time. A couple years later, I was able to upgrade to the Lunch Box monster truck. Playing with those cars were some of my fondest memories as a child. That's where all this shit started and stems from for me.

When I turned thirteen, I got a job at the local car wash on the corner of 183rd Street and 27th Avenue. I worked twelve-hour days—8:00 a.m. to 8:00 p.m.—for $30 a day plus tips. Seeing the dope boys pull into the car wash in their Benzes, I stopped caring about what type of toys I wanted for Christmas that year. I began dreaming about having the real thing. That desire motivated me to hustle harder. I started going above and beyond what was expected of me to try to earn extra tips. I'd vacuum up every crumb in those cars' interiors. I'd degrease the seats. I'd even organize people's cassette tapes in alphabetical order.

My passion for motor vehicles never went away. I believe that's a good thing. It speaks to my capacity for childlike wonderment. My OG Pablo Picasso once said that "Every child is an artist. The problem is how to remain an artist once we grow up."

What he's saying is that there's an innate creativity that can be found in all children. Then, as they grow older, a lot of people lose that youthful, wide-eyed spirit. We get told to grow up and to not be so childish. But childlike wonderment is an engine for creativity. It unlocks imagination. It drives exploration. It allows you to be brave and not care so much about other people's expectations of you or pressures from society. Those are all key components to creative thinking. Having a playful and inquisitive mindset is something to be embraced. Don't shy away from it.

I would go so far as to say that childlike wonderment is what led to the creation of the Barber Museum. Its founder, George Barber Jr., was the heir to Barber Dairies, which at one point was the largest dairy company in Alabama. But George Jr. wasn't all that interested in being a milkman. Like me, he was a motorsports enthusiast from a young age. He wanted to be a race car driver, and he was for over a decade. But when his daddy died, George Jr. had to hang up his racing helmet and take over the family business.

At first Mr. Barber tried to bring his need for speed into the dairy business. He started pulling up to grocery stores in his Ferrari. That didn't go over too well with his clients. This was the 1960s. He may have had the only Ferrari in Alabama at that time. Milk is a staple good for the common man, and Mr. Barber was coming off as anything but common in his flashy sportscar.

So, he turned in his red Ferrari for a white minivan and did what was best for business. That worked out pretty well for him. When he eventually sold Barber Dairies to Dean Foods in 1998, his company had annual revenues of over $200 million.

In 1995, a few years before he cashed out, he opened the first Barber Vintage Motorsports Museum in Birmingham's Southside neighborhood. But once he was out of the milk game, he went all in on what had always been his true passion. In 1997, he sent twenty-one of his motorcycles to the Guggenheim Museum in New York City as part of an exhibit called "The Art of the Motorcycle." Seeing his motorcycles inside a space as iconic as the Guggenheim got Mr. Barber's wheels turning (pun intended). He started envisioning something much bigger than what he had started in Southside Birmingham. Five years later, that vision came to fruition. The world-class complex that is the Barber Motorsports Park was born.

To say that I was impressed would be an understatement. That museum most definitely surpassed my expectations. As the tour came to a close, I thanked Robert and his staff for their hospitality and bought a few things from the gift shop to memorialize the visit. As I got back on the bus, my mind was racing with new ideas for my own collection and my annual car show at the Promise Land.

I needed a space like this, where I could properly showcase all my prized possessions. This was what I was missing. I had enough cars, so much so that I was running out of space to store them all. I needed to shift my focus from acquiring cars to displaying the ones I had. A few years back, I had torn down Holyfield's old boxing gym at the Promise Land and put up a warehouse in its place. But that was just for storage. I needed to think bigger. I needed to build my own car museum.

How much had it cost Mr. Barber to build his mecca for motorcycles? I looked it up. Sources said somewhere between $54 and $70 million. Somewhere between $30 to $40 million for the museum—and another $20 to $30 million for the racetrack and facilities. And all that money came straight out of Mr. Barber's pockets. The whole project was privately funded by him without any outside investors.

Well goddamn.

I can't say I was shocked. You get what you pay for in this country, and a complex of that caliber looks like it was worth every penny. But $70 million is nothing to sneeze at. Having just spent roughly that amount between my private jet and Star Island crib, I may have to plan on opening up my museum a little down the line. It's not like I'd be able to debut it at next year's car show. This would have to be a long-term project.

Back on the bus, I reached for the TV remote and pulled up YouTube. I wanted to see if there was anything about Mr. Barber on there. The man had earned my respect, and I wanted to learn everything I could about him.

The first thing that came up was a segment that had aired on Birmingham's local television station WVTM-TV. In an interview with the correspondent, Mr. Barber repeated a lot of what I'd learned about the museum during my visit. But at the end he said something that almost made me spit my drink out.

"Over eight hundred acres of land, a world-class racetrack, the world's largest collection of motorcycles and it all started with an $80-million donation from George Barber. But . . . you don't make a dime out of anything here?'

"Oh no," Mr. Barber responded. "I cannot. This is a foundation, and I'm not really allowed to participate in any earnings. This is not for profit."

I had a good laugh at that one. Creativity doesn't always come in the medium of a painting or a poem. Creativity is when you spend $80 million on your car and bike collection project and find a way to write it off as contributions to a nonprofit foundation. We call that creative accounting.

Mr. Barber was a man after my own heart. He and I had more in common than our love of cars and motorcycles. This shrewd motherfucker was a hustler like Rozay.

CHAPTER 13

DIGITAL DISTRACTIONS

AFTER WATCHING THE GEORGE BARBER interview, the YouTube algorithm automatically played another video, and then another and then another. It wasn't until my stomach started rumbling that I snapped out of my screen-induced dissociative state. I pulled back the curtains of the bus's windows. It was dark out. How much time had passed since we'd left the museum? What had I been watching this whole time? I couldn't tell you.

I wasn't sure where we were or what time it was. At least I knew where we were headed: my momma's house in Mississippi. That would be our last stop of the day. That was where I wanted to lie down for the night and catch up on sleep. My internal clock was still thrown off from the trip to Dubai.

Remember, it was the night of the election. I wanted to have my momma close in case that civil war broke out. I looked at my phone. It was eight o'clock. The polls were closed but it would be a while before the official results of the election were in.

"Buddy, how much longer we got?" I shouted from the back.

"About an hour and a half left."

My stomach rumbling let me know that that was too long to wait. My momma wouldn't be happy if I spoiled my appetite before I got there, but I did need a snack. I'd leave some room to enjoy her home cooking.

"Pull over at the next fast-food spot. Let's get something to eat."

A few minutes later, the bus pulled into a parking lot. I looked out the window. We were at Raising Cane's. I shook my head. As far as fast-food options go, Raising Cane's ain't a bad one. But for me personally, it's a conflict of interest. Everybody knows that when it comes to fried chicken, my brand loyalty has always belonged to Wingstop. I knew Buddy and I were still just getting to know each other. This was only day one of the trip, after all. I decided to give him the benefit of the doubt. He'd learn these things soon enough.

"How close is the nearest Wingstop?"

"Um, it looks like there's one twelve minutes away."

Damn. "Is it twelve minutes in the direction we're going, or is it twelve minutes out of the way?"

"Unfortunately, looks like it's twelve minutes back in the direction we just came from."

That settled that. Raising Cane's it was. My business partners would have to forgive me. If I'm being honest, they weren't cutting me a big enough check these days to justify me spending an extra twenty-four minutes on this bus today. My relationship with Wingstop hadn't been the same since its CEO Charlie Morrison resigned a couple years back. So if the paparazzi caught me eating a six-piece Caniac Combo on election night, so be it. That was just something we would all have to deal with in the morning. It wouldn't be the first time I got caught stepping out with a side piece. I wasn't too concerned about that happening, anyway. By the look of it, we were in the middle of nowhere.

By the time we arrived, I was eager to get off the bus. I'd been on it for hours. I'd smoked several joints. The back of this bus was starting to feel like that hypobaric chamber. So I hopped off with the rest of the crew and went into Raising Cane's. I needed to stretch my legs and get some fresh air.

This particular Raising Cane's location had a bunch of memorabilia hanging on its walls. A framed letterman jacket from the local high school's varsity football team. Who knew the Mooreville Troopers won the state championship in 2001? A bronze bust of an English bulldog, the mascot for Mississippi State University. A vintage concert flyer for an Elvis Presley performance at the Mississippi-Alabama Fair and Dairy Show on September 26, 1956. There was actually a whole bunch of Elvis-related shit on the wall. That's when I came to the realization that I was in Tupelo.

This was not my first time passing through Tupelo, Mississippi. Far from it, as a matter of fact. I was born just two just hours west of Tupelo in Clarksdale. I have many childhood memories of my family packing into my daddy's old Buick—we named it "Old Scrappy"—and making the fifteen-hour drive from South Florida to Clarksdale to visit my momma's side of the family. And every time we would make that trip, we went through Tupelo.

I hadn't realized we were in Tupelo when I asked Buddy to stop. The fact that I was here meant two things. First, it meant that I actually owned that Wingstop location that was twelve minutes away, and that I should have just gone there after all. More importantly, it meant that I was in the birthplace of the King of Rock and Roll, Elvis Aaron Presley.

I got my Caniac Combo and headed back to the bus.

"Buddy, how far away are we from Elvis's old crib?"

"About ten minutes."

"But which direction?"

"Back where we came from."

Goddamn Buddy. Not giving me the answers I wanted today.

I considered having him turn around so we could swing by the house, but it was pitch-black out and the official visiting hours had ended hours ago. We wouldn't be able to see shit anyway. Plus I didn't want to keep my momma up waiting for me.

"Forget it. Let's just keep going."

I was frustrated. I could have gotten a ten-piece for free *and* rode past Elvis's childhood home, but I had been too busy watching YouTube and scrolling social media on my phone to notice we were riding through Tupelo. If I hadn't gotten off the bus to go to Raising Cane's, it would have gone over my head completely. I started thinking maybe the tour bus had been a bad idea. I'd thought that me being comfortable and having someone else handle the driving would have freed my mind to be more present and take in the sights. But what it'd actually done was just enable me to spend more of my time and attention staring at a screen.

Don't get me wrong. Social media and streaming entertainment can be an incredible tool for creativity. Shit, I got the idea to climb Mount Kilimanjaro from my Instagram and the idea to take a road trip from a documentary trailer on Netflix. Every day I see and learn something new from social media. I get exposed to all different types of creative communities and can connect with my fans and other artists from all over the world.

If you follow me on social media, you know I put out a lot of daily content. Unlike a lot of celebrities, I don't have someone on my team whose job it is to handle that stuff. I do it all myself. And I enjoy doing it. I love waking up and picking out an outfit based on what car I plan on driving that day and posting a dope picture of it. That doesn't feel like work to me. It's fun. It's another outlet I get to express myself creatively through.

But lately I had begun to feel like my phone was taking from me more than it was giving. I know I'm not the only one who feels that way. All these Tweets and Reels and TikToks were fucking with my attention span. Great ideas take time and patience to come together. But if you're consuming nothing but bite-sized, rapid-fire, surface-level pieces of content, your brain slowly starts to lose its ability to come up with complex, fully developed creative ideas.

To be clear, creativity can most definitely spring from

exposure to new things. That's what this whole road trip was about. That's what a lot of this book is about. But creativity also comes out of stillness. Those quiet moments when you feel bored and your mind begins to wander, explore that empty space, and then suddenly, boom, the great idea appears seemingly out of nowhere.

Social media apps, podcasts, and an endless autoplay of streaming entertainment has effectively eliminated those quiet moments. They don't occur naturally anymore. Now anytime we're bored, we can just grab our phone and be met with endless options to distract ourselves. They are literally at our fingertips.

Fresh ideas need space in our minds to take root and grow. But that space doesn't exist if we are always overstimulated. How can we come up with innovative, original thoughts if we're just constantly absorbing other people's?

The other thing is there's just so much toxic shit on social media. I barely go on Twitter or X or whatever it's called these days. Elon fucked that shit up so bad. It's like as soon as he bought the company, all I started seeing on there were things that disrupted my peace. The Diddy allegations. The Epstein files. Death and warfare in Ukraine and the Middle East. The United States on the brink of an insurrection and constitutional crisis.

I can't blame it all on Elon. That's something strange about human nature. We'll turn our heads to stare at the wreckage of a car crash, but then ride on by some beautiful rose bushes and think nothing of it. The engineers at these tech companies are aware of this, and built algorithms that prey on that. The more time we spend on their apps, the more dollars go into their pockets, and they don't give a fuck if they need to flood our brains with horrifying and fear-inducing content to do that. Fear is the enemy of creativity. Creativity and progress happen when you have an open mind and feel brave enough to step outside your comfort zone to explore and take chances. More and more, social media makes me want to hunker down in my comfort zone and fortify that shit like Fort Knox.

There had to be a middle ground. I still wanted to tap into the creative benefits, but I needed to exercise willpower and resist the digital poison the algorithm was trying to feed me. I wasn't sure exactly how I was going to strike that balance yet, but I would commit to making a conscious effort to do so.

My pit stop in Tupelo had been uneventful, but at least it resulted in some introspection and a new resolution I could start working toward. It also informed what I wanted to do the next day. I wasn't tripping over not being able to see Elvis's little two-room shotgun shack on Tupelo's Old Saltillo Road. I now had something bigger in mind.

"Buddy, be ready to move first thing in the morning."

"Will do, boss. You know where you want to head to next?"

"I do. We're going to Graceland."

CHAPTER 14

THE KING AND I

London, England,
January
The weather, gray
The rain, thick
I wake up, depression all around me
Dark thoughts clouding my mind
And I open the drawer and I see two things
I see the warm Tod loafers
And I see the crisp cashmere socks
And I know that today is going to be a good day
A hundred dollars a sock
Two ankles, you do the math
Pull them on, socks on first, followed by the loafers
Then I know from that day, that week, that month, that year, that decade, that millennium
That we're going to be rich forever
Rich Forever

—Rick Ross, "London Skit," *Rich Forever* (2012)

I THOUGHT OF THAT SKIT OFF MY *RICH Forever* mixtape when I got up the next morning. I looked out the window and saw dark clouds and heavy rain. The kind of weather that makes you want to stay inside all day. I checked my phone and had an alert that Donald Trump had won the election. The weather felt fitting.

But like that British voice actor said, I still had to pull up my socks and lace up my sneakers. I was blessed to see another day. I couldn't sit around waiting for the clouds to clear and lift my mood. That's not how you change your state of mind. If you find yourself in a funk when you wake up in the morning, the best thing you can do is get up off your ass and try to make something happen. Rain or shine, I was going to Graceland.

I'm no stranger to Memphis. My sister, niece, and nephew have lived there for years. My momma's thirty minutes away in Mississippi. Her whole side of my family is in that general vicinity.

A lot of my favorite rappers are from Memphis, too. 8Ball & MJG. The whole Three 6 Mafia. The late, great Young Dolph. When it comes to trap music, Atlanta tends to get the lion's share of credit for putting the genre on the map. I can't argue with that. But when you take a closer look at the music that T.I., Young Jeezy, and Gucci Mane were making in the early 2000s, it's obvious how much of it was influenced by what DJ Paul and Juicy J were doing in the early '90s. That Memphis sound laid the foundation for a lot of the music that's popular today.

Long story short, I've got a lot of love for Bluff City. I have family there, I own businesses there, and I've been influenced by and worked with many artists from there. I've been to Beale Street. I've visited the National Civil Rights Museum at the Lorraine Motel, where Martin Luther King Jr. got shot. But in all my years of going to Memphis, I had never been to Graceland, the legendary estate of Elvis Presley. That ended today.

There were a few reasons I wanted to go to Graceland. First and foremost, I'd just heard so much about the place over the years. It's a National Historic Landmark. I also knew that Elvis was a flashy, extravagant motherfucker like myself and had a taste for the finer things. I already knew his crib as an adult would be full of all sorts of fly shit that I would appreciate.

But beyond that, I had also been thinking about the future of the Promise Land, especially after my visit to the Barber Museum the day before. Renovations were currently underway at my new crib on Star Island, and I planned on spending a lot more time there in Miami when those were finished. So now I was weighing my options: Would I continue to have the Promise Land be my primary residence, or would I go all in on turning it into an event venue and tourist attraction? I had even been approached about potentially transforming it into a golf course. I could turn the crib into a full-on clubhouse with a restaurant and locker rooms and the guest house could be used as a pro shop. I was still trying to figure out what the right play was. I figured visiting the most visited private home in the United States—aside from the White House—might give me some ideas.

Damn near everybody in my life tried to talk me out of buying the Promise Land. It was another one of my "crazy ideas." I thought it was a steal. The home's previous owner, former heavyweight boxing champion Evander Holyfield, reportedly spent $30 million when he built the property in 1994. I paid $5.8 million for it when I purchased it in 2014. At that price, I thought it was crazy for me *not* to buy it.

At the time, though, nobody else seemed to agree. Everybody else saw this real estate acquisition as a money pit. Holyfield had lost his house in foreclosure despite having earned more than $230 million over the course of his career. As I pursued the purchase, I realized everyone in my circle was worried that I might be destined to that same fate.

Holyfield was at the peak of his powers when he acquired the land and began building his estate. He was coming off extremely lucrative pay-per-view events against names like George Foreman, Larry Holmes, and Riddick Bowe, and had a super fight with Mike Tyson on the horizon. He had endorsement deals with Coca-Cola, K-Mart, and Microsoft. He even had his own video game on Sega Genesis. "The Real Deal" Holyfield was everywhere. But as the years went on and he aged out of his athletic prime, those pay-per-view checks and brand deals started to dry up. And behind the scenes, he'd made a bunch of bad business decisions. You can probably guess what came next. It's another tale as old as time. Former pro athlete goes broke.

In 2014, I was at the peak of *my* powers. My career was at an all-time high following the release of *Rich Forever* and *God Forgives, I Don't.* Maybach Music Group was the hottest record label in the game. I was just starting to find success in various ventures outside of music. Like Evander twenty years before, I was the reigning heavyweight champion.

But the rap game, like boxing, is a young man's sport, so I get why people had their reservations about me buying the property. The sticker price may have been cheap, relative to what Holyfield had spent, but the cost of operating and preserving a 235-acre estate was most definitely not. There had been extensive reports on how expensive it was. The price you pay to keep that many acres of grass manicured year-round can put a couple groundskeepers' kids through college. You can't escape that electricity bill either. In the summer, it's the air-conditioning. In the winter, it's the Christmas lights. In-ground swimming pools have a reputation for being a money pit for any homeowner, so you can imagine the cost when your pool is the largest residential pool in the United States.

But none of those things concerned me. I already had a vision for the Promise Land. Creativity is not just about painting a canvas or playing an instrument. At its core, creativity is really about thinking differently and seeing possibilities that other people can't see yet. It's about vision. And that most definitely applies to business. In my mind, I already knew the Promise Land would never be a money pit. I was going to turn this place into a money machine. I was going to fill this three-hundred-and-fifty-thousand-gallon pool with hundred-dollar bills and do a belly flop into it like Scrooge McDuck.

Sometimes, you just have to ignore all the naysayers or doubters. And that's what I did. Four years after I purchased the property, Columbia Pictures rented it out as a shooting location for the remake of *Superfly.* A few years later, Paramount Pictures did the same: they paid me $2.75 million to turn the Promise Land into Zamunda for *Coming 2 America* starring Eddie Murphy. Then I started hosting the Rick Ross Car & Bike Show in my front yard. After that, the Boss Up business conference for entrepreneurs. And of course, the Rick Ross Pool Party extravaganza. In the decade I've owned the Promise Land, I've already made my initial investment into it back several times over.

But as successful as I've been with my estate, I can't say it's anywhere near the level of Graceland. Not yet, at least. Graceland attracts more than six hundred and fifty thousand visitors and brings in more than $10 million in revenue annually, and it's easy to see why.

The economic impact on the city of Memphis is estimated to be $150 million per year, and the estate was recently valued at close to half a billion dollars. So, I still had room to grow at the Promise Land. I knew I could learn a thing or two from the King.

If I'm being honest, when I first pulled into the gates of Graceland, I was a little underwhelmed. The house is seventeen thousand square feet, and the entire place covers fourteen acres. That's not a small piece of property by any means, but it's no Promise Land. My crib is forty-five thousand square feet and now sits on over three hundred acres. (It was two hundred and thirty-five when I bought it in 2014, then I added an additional eighty-seven acres after the property next door went on the market.)

Regardless, any disappointment I may have first felt disappeared as soon as I stepped inside the house. The interior of the home was opulent and ostentatious. I was struck by how perfectly preserved everything was. The living room's cream-colored sofa and carpet were immaculate. Not one wine stain or speck of dust to be seen. I'd imagined it would be like walking into a museum full of old historic shit, but it didn't feel like that because everything still looked brand-new. The experience was closer to having gone into a time machine and being transported to a rich motherfucker's crib in 1974.

Inside the living room was a smaller alcove music room. Connecting them an entryway made of stained-glass windows depicting floor-to-ceiling peacocks. I stepped back, as per my usual method, and took it all in. Those jewel-toned peacocks activated a long-lost image that had been hidden away in some corner of my mind: the cover of Elvis's 1975 album *Promised Land*. On it he was wearing a white jumpsuit with an embroidered peacock design.

I don't know if I ever even listened to that album. It wouldn't surprise me if I'd just had a strong response to the image. As a visual person, I've always been drawn to dope cover art. When I first started buying records, I would always check for dope covers. Even the ones from genres or artists I didn't necessarily listen to. My first LP was Run-DMC's *Raising Hell*, which I bought strictly based off the cover. When I saw the cover of *The 2 Live Crew Is What We Are*, where Luke had the Jeep Cherokee parked in front of the Pac Jam with "Luke Skywalker" printed on it, I just had to have it.

So I couldn't tell you one song off that Elvis album, and it wasn't far-fetched to think that I'd simply come across it in a record store once and the image of that peacock jacket had just stuck with me. The fact that it was titled *Promised Land* was certainly an interesting coincidence.

"I guess this flamboyant motherfucker Elvis really liked peacocks," I said out loud to no one in particular.

One of the Elvis superfans in attendance overheard my remark and chimed in.

"Well, at first he did," he told me. "Believe it or not, there were peacocks here at Graceland. But what happened was they started pecking the paint off Elvis's beloved gold Cadillac, so he had them banished from the property. He ended up donating them to the Memphis Zoo."

Ain't that some shit. Those birds got off easy if you

ask Rozay. If that had happened to one of my old-school Chevys, me and my homies would have been eating peacock stew for supper.

Sitting inside the music room was Elvis's grand piano. It was white with gold accents, and tucked underneath it was a custom leather bench. The superfan informed me that Elvis used to hold court in there for hours, playing the piano for family and friends as they gathered around him.

The dining room also had white carpet, but in the middle, right underneath the dining table and chairs was black marble tile. I liked the contrast of that design choice. As far as the actual table went though, I think I had Elvis beat. I'd recently had a custom brunch table made from the turbine of a Boeing 757 airplane. I know the King would have loved it.

Elvis's kitchen was a time capsule of the '70s. Carpet in every room. Floor-to-ceiling wood paneling. All the retro appliances were in pristine condition. Elvis even had a microwave oven, which according to my new friend was extremely rare in those days.

"That is the first microwave ever sold in the city of Memphis," he whispered.

I liked this guy, and I liked the information he was providing me. Graceland needed to hire this gentleman. Better yet, I thought, maybe I should catch him up to speed on all my artifacts and hire him to lead tours at the Promise Land. I could be looking at my future museum director.

From there, we made our way downstairs to the TV room, which featured a bold yellow-and-navy-blue color scheme that would make any fan of the Michigan Wolverines proud. It reminded me that somewhere I had a limited-edition pair of Air Jordan 3s in the exact same colorway. They even had Michigan's block-style "M" logo embroidered on the tongue. I remember wishing I had those sneakers on right then. I could have gotten a hard photo of me kicking it in Elvis's TV room. Where were those sneakers anyway?

There were three television sets mounted on the walls. The same exact setup I have at the Promise Land. My buddy told me that Elvis got the idea from former President Lyndon Johnson, who used it to watch all three network news programs simultaneously. Where had I gotten the idea from? I couldn't recall. But it just goes to show: no idea's original.

The TV room was striking, no doubt about it. But the pool room next door? That made the TV room look tame. The walls, ceilings, even the couches were all completely covered with this bright, multicolored pleated fabric. I felt like I was inside of a circus tent. I couldn't believe Elvis had a fucking fireplace in this room. Somebody may need to call the fire marshal about that. If this was my crib, one wrong flick of my joint could make this whole place burst into flames.

The second floor of the house—where Elvis's master suite is—remains off-limits to the public. So the last stop inside the main house was the infamous Jungle Room. This was the attraction I'd always heard about—and let me tell you, it lived up to the hype. It was a tropical man

cave, complete with moss-like green shag pile carpet on the floor and ceiling and a built-in rock waterfall on the wall. I grabbed for my phone and called up my contractor who was overseeing the renovations back on Star Island.

"I want an indoor rock waterfall," I told him, "and I want an indoor koi pond. We'll discuss the details when I get back."

I headed out the back door and found myself in Elvis's backyard. From there I had a couple different options. Straight ahead was the office of Elvis's pops, Vernon Presley. Across the yard was the Trophy Building, and opposite that was the racquetball center. What I really wanted to do was go say what's up to Elvis's horses, who I could see roaming in the nearby paddock. Elvis and I were both equestrian enthusiasts. Another thing we had in common.

Unfortunately it was still raining pretty hard, so I would have to catch the ponies another time. Instead I decided to go check out the other spots. I have a few extra buildings at the Promise Land that I still haven't found a good purpose for. What used to be Holyfield's guest house had remained a storage unit for my overflow of items. If Elvis could give me a couple ideas of what to do with these additional spaces, that might be the motivation I needed to get my hoarding issue under control.

Attached to the door of Vernon Presley's office was a sign. In big, bold letters it read:

PLEASE READ AND OBSERVE:
NO LOAFING IN OFFICE
STRICTLY FOR **EMPLOYEES**
ONLY! IF YOU HAVE BUSINESS
HERE. PLEASE TAKE CARE
OF IT AND LEAVE
—Vernon Presley

Elvis's pops was about his business. He handled all the paperwork so his son could focus on what he did best: music and acting. I couldn't help but think about my sister and all the things she takes care of on a daily basis so that I don't have to. All the little tasks and assignments that I'll never even know about. I don't know what I'd do without her.

Out of respect for Vernon's wishes, I decided I didn't need to go any further. Do I look like a nigga who walks into a place of business and starts loafing? I refused to be a loafer. The only loafers I cosign with are the ones designed by Gucci. As soon as I got back, I decided, I was getting my own "No Loafing" sign for my in-home recording studio.

Elvis had gone all in on racquetball, which in the '70s was the fastest-growing sport in the country. By this point, it should come as no surprise that this spot was more than just a court. It was a whole pimped-out recreational facility. Behind the court's floor-to-ceiling shatterproof window was a viewing area with dark leather couches, a pinball machine, a bar, and even a piano, just in case inspiration struck Elvis after playing some racquetball with his "Memphis Mafia" crew.

I never played racquetball, but I had been meaning to take up pickleball. Pickleball was now having a similar surge in popularity to racquetball's in the '70s. Just a few weeks before, I had approved a sample clearance for "Hustlin'" to be featured in a Michelob Ultra Super Bowl commercial starring Willem Dafoe and Catherine O'Hara, where they school some youngsters on the pickleball court. I already had a court and paddles at the Promise Land. What was I waiting for?

The amount of Gold and Platinum plaques in Elvis's Trophy Building was something else. We're talking about the bestselling solo artist of all time, with an estimated one billion records sold worldwide. The Trophy Building also had his legendary stage outfits on display. Posters from his thirty-three movie appearances. Every type of cool artifact and piece of Elvis memorabilia that you could imagine. My mind went back to my museum idea. I could have more than just my cars. It could showcase all my many passions and the treasures and keepsakes I've acquired over the course of my life.

Like the Lotus 49 replica at the Barber Museum, I came across something in Graceland's Trophy Building that stopped me in my tracks. Something inside a display case caught my eye. As I approached, I saw a Colt .45 semiautomatic pistol inside. It had custom handle grips made from turquoise, jagged little pieces of gemstone that fit together like a puzzle. It was a beautiful firearm, and apparently it was Elvis's favorite. I could see why.

Displayed above the gun was an identification card:

STATE OF COLORADO
ORGANIZED CRIME STRIKE FORCE
THIS IDENTIFIES
ELVIS PRESLEY, CAPTAIN
OF
Denver Police Department
AS
Investigator

It was one of many honorary badges on display in the room. As I scanned the ID I saw that this particular one was issued by J.D. McFarlane, the former Attorney General of Colorado. And it was dated January 28, 1976.

That couldn't be right. I did a double take, and sure enough, it was the day I was born. Down to the exact year. This shit was a Twilight Zone moment.

What the fuck was going on here? What was up with all these strange coincidences? The amount of synchronicity that was happening here was overwhelming. This was starting to feel like my bad mushroom trip when I thought I was the runaway slave from *Emancipation*.

What was I supposed to take from all this? Was I the modern-day Elvis? If I was, what did that mean?

Elvis Presley lived a hell of a life, and Graceland was an estate like no other. But I had seen both the *Elvis* and *Priscilla* movies, so I knew that Elvis's story was a bit more complicated. The King went out sad at the end. Depressed. Lonely. Paranoid. Addicted to drugs. On August 16, 1977, he was found unresponsive on the floor of his bathroom here at Graceland. Dead from a heart attack brought on by long-term substance abuse and terrible eating habits. He was only forty-two years old.

I left the Trophy Building and headed back out into the rain. The energy of my visit to Graceland had shifted. There was a heaviness to it now. I could feel it as I approached the last stop of the tour. The Meditation Garden, Elvis's final resting place. I looked down at the headstone.

ELVIS AARON PRESLEY
JANUARY 8, 1935
AUGUST 16, 1977
SON OF
VERNON ELVIS PRESLEY
AND
GLADYS LOVE PRESLEY
FATHER OF
LISA MARIE PRESLEY

HE WAS A PRECIOUS GIFT FROM GOD
WE CHERISHED AND LOVED DEARLY.
HE HAD GOD-GIVEN TALENT THAT HE SHARED
WITH THE WORLD. AND WITHOUT A DOUBT,
HE BECAME MOST WIDELY ACCLAIMED:
CAPTURING THE HEARTS OF YOUNG AND OLD ALIKE.
HE WAS ADMIRED NOT ONLY AS AN ENTERTAINER,
BUT AS THE GREAT HUMANITARIAN THAT HE WAS:

FOR HIS GENEROSITY, AND HIS KIND FEELINGS
FOR HIS FELLOW MAN.
HE REVOLUTIONIZED THE FIELD OF MUSIC AND
RECEIVED ITS HIGHEST AWARDS.
HE BECAME A LIVING LEGEND IN HIS OWN TIME,
EARNING THE RESPECT AND LOVE OF MILLIONS.
GOD SAW THAT HE NEEDED SOME REST AND
CALLED HIM HOME TO BE WITH HIM
WE MISS YOU, SON AND DADDY. I THANK GOD
THAT HE GAVE US YOU AS OUR SON
—VERNON PRESLEY

To the left lay the headstone for Minnie Mae Presley, Elvis's grandmother. His parents, Vernon and Gladys, were to his right. On the other side of the fountain across from Elvis were two other above-ground tombs, one for Elvis's daughter, Lisa Marie Presley, and next to her, her son Benjamin Keough. Elvis's grandson had died at the age of twenty-seven.

I boarded the shuttle, and we headed toward "Elvis Presley's Memphis," a two-hundred-thousand-square-foot entertainment and exhibit complex. There was a lot left of the Elvis experience waiting for us there: the Presley Motors automobile museum, and Elvis Presley's "Flying Graceland," where his private planes are on display. Normally those would be the things that I would be most excited to check out. But I decided I was ready to call it a day. I'd seen enough cars. Graceland had given me a lot to think about.

CHAPTER

15

CREATIVE COLLABORATION

ON THE ONE HAND, VISITING THE BARBER Museum and Graceland had been dope. Both places were right up my alley, and I'd gotten back on the bus with all sorts of new ideas for the Promise Land and my car museum. On the other hand, something about being in Elvis's Meditation Garden and being confronted with his grave had left me with deeper existential questions about the meaning of life. Were my own passions and pursuits so shallow and trivial? Was all of it—the flash, the extravagance, the fly shit—really worth it for the King in the end? Was it worth it for me?

We were on the way to Hot Springs, Arkansas, where we would stop for the night. My sister had booked us an Airbnb overlooking Lake Hamilton. She had recently vacationed in Hot Springs, and from what I'd heard, it sounded like a cool spot, even if we would be there in the dead of November.

The area is located in the Ouachita Mountains of Western Arkansas. People were drawn to the region's naturally flowing hot springs long before it became a formal city. Way before the Europeans arrived, Native American tribes called it the "Valley of the Vapors" and revered the hot springs, which they believed to contain healing and restorative powers.

Centuries later, Hot Springs became a popular destination and a safe haven for reputed mobsters like Al Capone, Lucky Luciano, Bugsy Siegel, and Frank Costello. They started coming down here for more than just the springs. The city had built a reputation for being an openly corrupt gambling town, with casinos, horse racing, prostitution, and underground bootlegging. With the local authorities in the pocket of these organized crime figures, it was the perfect place to lie low whenever there was too much heat on them at home.

Those things were of interest to me. I had been looking forward to soaking in the hot springs and reaping any of its supposed medicinal and spiritual benefits. I also wanted to check out the Ohio Club, as well as the Arlington Hotel, where Capone would rent out the entire fourth floor. Legend has it he had a secret escape route through a door in his closet that led to an underground tunnel network underneath the city's downtown.

Unfortunately, I wasn't going to be able to do any of those things. The "Al Capone Suite" at the Arlington Hotel was booked, and the delayed start to the road trip had put us behind schedule. The consequence was that we now had to cover more distance each day in order to get to Las Vegas in time for my show. More hours on the road meant fewer hours for activities and exploration.

By the time we arrived at the Airbnb, it was a little after 10:00 p.m. And we had to get back on the road first thing Thursday morning. I was starting to regret taking that last-minute show in Dubai. Was that extra bag of oil money really worth it?

The Airbnb was first-class, though. A six-bedroom lakefront retreat with a hot tub, a home movie theater, and a game room with pool and Ping-Pong tables. There was even a *PAC-MAN* arcade machine. But I wasn't interested in any of those amenities. I had Joanne give me a quick foot massage and then retired to my room for the night.

I got up early the next morning. I wanted to take in the view of Lake Hamilton before we headed out. After throwing on a hoodie, I walked down toward the shoreline, where I found a seat in an Adirondack chair. I closed my eyes and inhaled the scent of the pine trees all around me. I felt the damp earth underneath my feet. Then, sparking a joint, I looked out onto the lake. A great blue

heron descended over the water, gliding across the surface. I was grateful to bear witness to it.

I could have stayed in that chair and watched the birds fly by all day, but I didn't have that luxury. We had a long day ahead of us. The next stop was Amarillo, Texas, and that was nine hours away, not counting any pit stops for gas and food. I was going to be stuck on this damn bus all day.

I took my seat in the back. My first impulse was to reach for the TV remote. I caught myself, and then had to resist the urge to substitute the remote with my phone. I wasn't falling into that trap again. Instead, I opened the curtains of the bus window and looked out at the Ouachita Mountains.

The trees were in full fall foliage. There were pockets of red, orange, and yellow tucked among the trees. In a week or two, all those leaves would be on the ground. Thank God I didn't just get on the bus and start watching YouTube videos again. I'd already found a better use of my time: taking in the beauty of the sights we were passing through. Eventually, Neil came into the back lounge.

"Let's talk about the book. Have you given any more thought to what else you want to share about your creative process? I was thinking we could get into your ear for beats."

My ear for beats. As far as writing prompts go, it was a decent one. Why not? Let's talk about it.

I actually wasn't familiar with the phrase "ear for beats" until I noticed it kept appearing in my album reviews. Over time, it's become one of the most frequently recurring comments I get on my music. Early on in my career, I wasn't sure what to make of it. I wasn't even sure that it was a compliment.

I don't typically read my album reviews. It can be a weird experience reading a music critic's analysis of your work and then seeing it graded on a scale of one to ten or however many stars or whatever. Even the positive reviews will contain at least some criticism, and I tend to hold on to that one negative remark more than the praise. Whenever I do read an album review, I'm usually on high alert, waiting for that moment when the writer will inevitably turn on me. Music critics can be some snarky motherfuckers. One minute they're praising your abilities and then a few sentences later they're twisting the knife in your back.

That's why I was wary at first about the whole "ear for beats" thing. Was this some sort of backhanded compliment? Like the subtext was that my skills as a writer and rapper were subpar, so any dope music I was making was just due to me having picked great beats? Were these writers on some passive-aggressive shit? But that was all early on in my career, when I was a little more paranoid and hypervigilant. With time, I grew to take the compliment for what it was. I take pride in my ear for beats.

> "It's well known that Ross' ear for beats is immaculate."
>
> —*HotNewHipHop*

> "The best Rick Ross is when his golden ear for beats finds a gem for his charismatic flow to float over."
>
> —*DJBooth*

> "Ross' ear for lush, expansive beats has become keener and his industry Rolodex deeper, allowing him to make every track but the intro feel like an epic . . ."
>
> —Simon Vozick-Levinson, *Entertainment Weekly*

> "He's been one of the most respected MCs in the game since he came into it, part owing to a billion dollar voice, an ability to convey the most luxurious lifestyle with brilliant word play, and an impeccable ear for beats."
>
> —Mark Ronson, *The FADER Uncovered Podcast*

I shouldn't undersell myself. I don't just have a great ear for beats. According to Mark Ronson when I appeared on his podcast in 2021, I have an *impeccable* ear for beats.

Even if you don't know who Mark Ronson is, I can assure you with a high degree of certainty that you are familiar with his work. Anybody who tells you they've never heard the song "Uptown Funk," the longest-running number one hit of the 2010s, is either lying to you or a doomsday prepper who's been living in an underground bunker for the past ten years. Either way, they're not to be trusted.

I know what some of you are thinking: "'Uptown Funk'? Ain't that a Bruno Mars record?" I can understand why you'd think that. After all, Bruno's voice is the one you hear on the song. But go pull up the credits. "Uptown Funk" is officially a song by music producer Mark Ronson *featuring* Bruno Mars. Eleven times Platinum, "Uptown Funk" is the biggest hit of Mark Ronson's career (and Bruno's), but it's most definitely not his only one. This British motherfucker is a nine-time Grammy winner and one of the most critically acclaimed and commercially successful music producers of the twenty-first century. It was an honor to speak to him on his podcast, and being told that I have an "impeccable ear for beats" from someone like him can only be taken as a compliment.

So how did I end up with this phenomenal ear for beats? Was I born with an especially large cochlea? Is there something unique about my auditory system? If so, my momma never told me about it. But I do have a few thoughts on the role it plays in my work.

At the most basic level, the music I make contains two elements: vocals and beats. Call it instrumentation or production or whatever you want. I'm of the firm belief that those two elements are equally important to the quality of a record. To me, this has always been obvious. But a lot of recording artists, and maybe rappers in particular, don't realize that. I put as much energy into the rhythm of my music as I put toward writing the lyrics. My ear for beats is a result of me placing such a high value on production. The way I see it, picking the right beat is actually half my job. If I'm working with the highest-quality ingredients, it's hard for me to go wrong from there.

The emphasis I place on production also speaks to how important I think collaboration is to the creative process. Let's go back to "Uptown Funk" for a second. That song is a very rare exception, where the producer is credited as the lead artist and the vocalist is the featured artist. That's almost never the case. The performer of the song is the one who tends to get most of the credit for a song's success. Producers' contributions can easily get forgotten about. Just a few paragraphs ago, I had to make sure you all knew who Mark Ronson was. Had it been Bruno Mars talking about my ear for beats, I would not have felt the same need to give such an introduction.

I'm not saying every producer and beatmaker deserves to be on magazine covers and billboards and get the same amount of shine as lead performers. That's not the point I'm trying to make here. Things like stage presence, charisma, and star power matter, and that's why guys like Bruno Mars usually end up getting most of the limelight.

The real problem is when the fans aren't the only ones who overlook the importance of the producer. Artists end up doing it too. Once they lose sight of that, they spend less time and attention on their production, and the result is shittier beats and shittier music.

When you team up with people who come from different backgrounds and disciplines and have their own sets of skills that complement yours, you expand the limits of what you're capable of creating on your own. Your ideas go further.

I'm not just talking about working with other artists or producers. Look at the success of my partnership with Brett Berish on Luc Belaire and Sovereign Brands. Look at my track record working with Neil on these books. One of my favorite expressions is "your network determines your net worth." You can apply that to basically any type of venture.

I've never collaborated with Mark Ronson, but I know if I did, we would make something legendary. I have, however, shared a stage with Bruno Mars before. Talk about a magic moment of creative collaboration. In 2011, I was blessed to have the opportunity to perform alongside Alicia Keys and Bruno Mars at the BET Awards. I stood backstage and watched as the two of them paired their dynamic vocal talents for a duet rendition of Alicia's classic song "A Woman's Worth." As the song reached its end, Alicia switched gears and began to sing T-Pain's opening hook on my song "Maybach Music 2."

> Hey, realest shit I ever wrote, chillin' in my Maybach
> Whatever I send out, homie, I'ma make back
> Can you believe it?
> You gotta see it
> 'Cause I don't plan on goin' broke, put that on my
> Maybach

'Cause I'm in it to win now, niggas can't take that
Listen to my Maybach Music
To my Maybach Music

Then I emerged from the back and took center stage, backed by Alicia fucking Keys on the piano and Bruno fucking Mars on his electric guitar.

Kush burn like petroleum
Crib needs custodians
Shades in all shades
These made of rhodium

That moment was made possible by Alicia Keys, Bruno Mars, and I coming together, each of us bringing our own set of gifts and talents to the table to collectively create something special.

That moment also wouldn't have been possible without the contributions from my homies J.U.S.T.I.C.E. League, who produced the "Maybach Music 2" beat, or T-Pain, Kanye West, and Lil' Wayne, who appeared on the original version of the song. When J.U.S.T.I.C.E. League first played me that beat, I never could have guessed how far that connection—that little spark—would eventually travel.

Creativity thrives on collaboration, regardless of whether it's for a can't-miss one-night-only performance or a classic record that stands the test of time.

CHAPTER 16

FORTUNE FAVORS THE BRAVE

THE STUNNING MOUNTAIN SCENERY DIDN'T last long. Within an hour we were getting on the flat and featureless Interstate 40, where we would remain for the next eight hours. With nothing but time and road ahead of us, Neil and I continued our conversations about my work, unraveling different aspects of the creative process. Some of the substance of those discussions has already been incorporated into earlier chapters of this book, and there's still more to come.

I realize I'm breaking the fourth wall of the bookmaking process, but I'm just trying to keep it real with my readers. As a matter of fact, in the spirit of keeping it real, I need to be fully transparent: on this bus trip, I may have taken a brief intermission from our book brainstorming sessions to watch the recently released documentary *The Menendez Brothers* on Netflix. This was not me regressing to the errors of my past ways or the same thing as falling into a social media black hole. You've got to trust me on this one. There was nothing to see on this stretch of the trip.

When I put on the show, Neil left the lounge to go lie down in the bus's bunkhouse for a few. Not long after, I checked my phone, and he'd sent me a bunch of texts. I opened up my messages and saw they were links to breaking news articles, including from the *New York Times*:

Several Feet of Snow Are Expected in New Mexico and Colorado

". . . meteorologists said could be the worst blizzard to hit the region in decades . . ."

". . . dangerous road conditions and power outages . . ."

". . . warned residents to delay travel plans . . ."

Plus other headlines from the Associated Press and CNN:

New Mexico governor declares emergency as western winter storm leaves thousands without power

About 100 vehicles stranded in rural New Mexico in below-freezing conditions during 'powerful' snowstorm

Damn. It might be a wrap for this road trip. We wouldn't have any trouble getting to Amarillo tonight, but tomorrow's forecast was looking crazy. And tomorrow was supposed to be the grand finale of the trip before we got to Vegas on Saturday. The plan had been to go to Santa Fe, where we had made arrangements to participate in a sacred Native American sweat lodge ceremony. But the way this shit was looking, we weren't going to be able to get to Santa Fe. We would have to drive through "the worst blizzard to hit the region in decades."

Neil came back into the lounge and slumped onto the couch. I passed him a joint. I could tell my dawg was stressing. He didn't know how we were going to pull a book out of this adventure without the climax in Santa Fe. I wasn't sure either.

However this was going to shake out, I knew the trip wasn't a complete loss. My experiences had most definitely gotten my creative gears turning again and helped me start to shake off the fog I'd been in. I would be coming home with some fresh ideas. But I would be lying if I said this wasn't a letdown. To end this shit in Amarillo would feel anticlimactic. I'd been hoping for a full-on spiritual and creative awakening at the sweat lodge ceremony. It seemed like we weren't going to get that grand finale.

At approximately 10:00 p.m., more than twelve hours after we'd departed from Hot Springs, our bus pulled into Amarillo's Big Texan Steak Ranch. You can't miss this place. Right off I-40, it's the bright yellow building with a sixty-foot-tall neon cowboy sign out front.

I stepped outside, and the first thing I encountered was a two-story-high cow statue made out of fiberglass. Behind me was an even bigger one of an alligator. He seemed to be an authority figure of some sort. Like he was watching over the parking lot. Just what type of establishment was this? They do say everything is bigger in Texas.

The Big Texan Steak Ranch is one of Amarillo's two

main attractions. We'll get to the second one later. The Big Texan Steak Ranch is famous for its over-the-top, Wild West–themed signage and decor. Joanne called it kitschy. That was a new word I learned that evening.

The Big Texan Steak Ranch's claim to fame is its seventy-two-ounce Steak Dinner Challenge: if you can finish a seventy-two-ounce steak, as well as a shrimp cocktail, baked potato, and salad, in under an hour, you get it all for free. Participants are seated in a specific area in the middle of the restaurant so they can be watched—fishbowl-style—engorging themselves to oblivion by the other patrons. It's also livestreamed to the internet. This shit was quite the spectacle.

I wasn't feeling up for the seventy-two-ounce steak dinner. Neither was anyone else in the crew. I wished Slab or Kano had been there. I would have coerced one of them through bribery to do that shit for my entertainment.

Team morale was pretty low. Everybody was physically drained from having spent the entire day on the bus. Our legs were stiff. Our backs were tight. I think mentally we were all a little confused too. We hadn't yet figured out what we were going to do the next day. As a group, we all decided to get our food to go and eat back at the hotel where we were spending the night.

I told Joanne my order—the eight-ounce top sirloin, a piece of fried fish, a garden salad, and a slice of carrot cake—and then began to wander around the strange

saloon-themed establishment. The place was a fever dream.

Inside the gift shop, I encountered a real seven-foot diamondback rattlesnake sitting inside a terrarium, who the cashier introduced as "Debra." Directly next to the gift shop was a shooting gallery. I sat down on a saddle and shot at various critters and creatures. Next to that was a penny press machine that flattened and elongated pennies and stamped them with the restaurant's logo.

I pressed me up a penny and kept it moving. And then I came face-to-face with Zoltar.

If you're not familiar with Zoltar, let me break it down for you real quick. Zoltar is a coin-operated fortune-teller machine that features a life-size mechanical gypsy inside a glass case. You give Zoltar the money and he grants you some kind of wish. I recognized Zoltar from the 1988 Tom Hanks film *Big*, where a young boy wishes to be grown-up and Zoltar turns him into Tom Hanks. I'd never seen a Zoltar in real life though. Was this *that* Zoltar? He couldn't be. This had to be like when you go to the mall to take pictures with Santa. You know he's not the real Santa. It's just some fat motherfucker in a costume.

I decided to not question Zoltar's authenticity. Instead, more curious than anything, I put a dollar into the machine. As soon as I did, his mechanical mouth started talking to me.

> "My name is Zoltar the Gypsy and I have some words of wisdom to bring you much happiness. As you travel through this life, remember this: if

you think you can or you think you can't, you're right! Go ahead and let Zoltar tell you more."

Man, fuck Zoltar. If I think I can or I think I can't, I'm right? Who hasn't heard that bullshit a million times?

I came to Zoltar in search of some words of inspiration in a moment of uncertainty. I couldn't believe that played-out cliché was all he had to offer. I wanted my dollar back. If it weren't for his glass encasement separating us, I would have slapped the shit out of Zoltar. I bet that glass wasn't bulletproof. I decided to get back on the bus before I caught a charge in Amarillo.

As I turned away and started to head for the exit, I heard a sound that stopped me. The machine spit out a yellow card. I turned back to Zoltar and pulled it out. What else could this motherfucker possibly have to say?

YOUR FORTUNE

Stop worrying about what is beyond your control and start focusing on what is. Some things are just written in the stars, my friend. Now is the time to step back and watch your life unfold before your eyes. Some of the best things happen when you least expect it.

CHAPTER 17

CADILLAC RANCH

FRIDAY WAS SUPPOSED TO BE A LIGHT TRAVEL day. Under normal circumstances, the drive from Amarillo to Santa Fe is a little over four hours. The plan had been to get there in the early afternoon, with plenty of time to grab lunch and check into our hotel before the sweat lodge ceremony later that evening, which was scheduled for 5:00 p.m.

But when I woke up Friday morning and got back on the bus, the question wasn't whether or not we would still make it to Santa Fe on time. It seemed like a foregone conclusion we wouldn't be able to get there at all, and that it would be extremely dangerous for us to even attempt to do so. It would require us to drive directly into one of the worst early-season snowstorms in decades.

The National Weather Service had issued winter storm warnings in Colorado, New Mexico, Oklahoma, and Texas, with over two feet of snow being forecast in some places.

"Travel will be impossible on almost all roads. Do not travel. Life-threatening conditions will exist."

We'd only seen rain so far—no snow—and I wasn't ready to pull the plug just yet. There was something telling me to let the situation play out a little longer. I let

Buddy know that for now, we were sticking with the original plan.

"Okay, boss. You got it."

We hadn't been on the road for more than ten minutes when Buddy pulled over. Was he folding on me already? Could I really blame him if he was?

Buddy wasn't giving up quite yet. There really ain't too much going on in Amarillo, so if you are passing through, the Big Texan Steak Ranch and Cadillac Ranch are the two main places you want to check out. I looked out the window and saw that Buddy had pulled over because we had arrived at Cadillac Ranch, Amarillo's second claim to fame.

It wasn't snowing in Amarillo yet. Honestly, I would have preferred snow to the conditions I was seeing from the bus window. Here we were being treated to heavy thunderstorms and fifty-mile-per-hour gusts of wind.

I had not packed appropriately for this. No boots. No rain jacket. No long johns. My nigga, I didn't even have a fucking umbrella. I asked Buddy if he happened to have a pair of binoculars so I could peep this Cadillac Ranch shit from the comfort of a dry and temperature-controlled tour bus—but no luck.

If I had any faith that the road trip would carry on as planned, I would have told Buddy to keep driving. We could skip the Cadillac Ranch. But it was starting to feel like the end was near. If that was the case, I didn't want it to end like this, with me squinting out the window to see Cadillac Ranch from two hundred yards away because I didn't have the heart to get off the bus and brave the elements.

Outside it is.

As soon as I stepped off the bus, my white, fresh-out-of-the-box Nike Air Force 1's were submerged in mud. On my jet, I have a shoe cover machine that everyone has to step into upon boarding. It wraps your shoes in a clear plastic wrap to keep outside dirt and debris from contaminating my aircraft. This felt like that, except when I lifted my shoe, instead of it being protected, it was completely caked in brown sludge.

Goddamn.

Cadillac Ranch is a public art installation. Built in 1974, it consists of a row of ten old-school Cadillacs buried nose-first in a former cornfield located off Route 66. The sixty-degree angle at which they're buried makes it look like they came from outer space and crashed into the earth at a high velocity.

The ten models, from 1949 to 1963, all feature the iconic Cadillac tailfin. Many car enthusiasts consider the 1950s and '60s to be the "golden age" of American automobile manufacturing and design. Put me down as one of those people. I was very familiar with the tailfin era. A few years back, I'd acquired a pink 1959 Cadillac Eldorado convertible. Her tailfin back is so damn big I named her BBL.

Cadillac wasn't the only one putting tailfins on their cars. General Motors was putting them on their Chevrolet Bel Airs and Impalas too. As a proud owner of more than two hundred motor vehicles, it's hard to pick a favorite. I love them all. But if someone put a pistol to my dome and I had to pick one, it would be my 1957 Bel Air. That answer is a bit of a copout considering I own close to twenty different variations of the '57 Chevy, but let's not argue over semantics. My preference for the convertible versus the hard top depends on the weather, and my preference for color depends on the outfit I'm wearing on that particular day. Suffice to say, I wouldn't pull any of them out under these conditions. I'm getting sidetracked. Back to Cadillac Ranch.

The cars were installed in their original factory paint jobs but were quickly defaced and covered in graffiti. Today, fifty years since its construction, all the cars are coated in countless layers of spray paint.

There's no ticket office at Cadillac Ranch. No plaque. No tour guide posted up whose job it is to explain the history of the installation or the meaning behind it. No security to prevent vandals from tagging it up. It's just some fly-looking shit on the roadside in the middle of Texas that anyone is welcome to stop by and add their own mark to.

The original idea for Cadillac Ranch came out of Ant Farm, a crew of avant-garde artists and architects. Ant Farm member Hudson Marquez was a car fanatic who was always drawing cars and making collages out of car advertisements in magazines. Talk about embracing some childlike wonderment.

Marquez's first idea was to design and print fake seed packets that featured cars growing out of the soil and then place them in stores alongside real seed packets for flowers or vegetables.

"The whole idea was to get someone to look through and ask the feedstore guy, 'What in tarnation is this?'" Marquez told *Artsy*.

The idea expanded after Ant Farm connected with an eccentric millionaire from Amarillo named Stanley Marsh. Mr. Marsh could see these guys were onto something but he had a bigger vision. And he was willing to cut them a check to bring that vision to life.

"Why don't we just do that for real?" Marquez recalled Marsh telling him. "I said 'Grow cars? You mean like a Cadillac ranch?' And Stanley said, 'That's it!'"

That's how the idea for Cadillac Ranch came to be.

To me, the Cadillac Ranch origin story speaks to some of the most important elements of the creative process. The way creative ideas start out, with artists drawing from their own personal interests and hobbies. The way the "seeds" of those initial ideas develop naturally and can change significantly over time before reaching their final form. The power of collaboration and what's possible when different creative minds join forces, which we discussed earlier.

Cadillac Ranch is also an example of how art has different meanings to different people. To the gearheads at Ant Farm, the installation was a pretty straightforward tribute to Cadillac's tailfin era. To Stanley Marsh, it had a different significance.

> "Cadillac Ranch is a monument to the American Dream. And the dream of most American boys when I was growing up . . . was to get a Cadillac, or a car of any kind. A car represented money. It was the first valuable thing we ever had. It represented sex, and it represented getting away from home. And I assure you those were the three things that were on our mind when we were sixteen."

Bruce Springsteen, the only other biggest Boss I recognize, wrote a song about this place. In his view, the Cadillac Ranch wasn't a ranch at all. It was more of a Cadillac cemetery. A graveyard. A metaphor for the final destination on the long, strange, and winding road of life. It represents our mortality and the passage of time.

Well buddy, when I die, throw my body in the back
And drive me to the junkyard in my Cadillac

—Bruce Springsteen, "Cadillac Ranch," *The River* (1980)

The cars were more than two hundred yards away from where we pulled over. These may have been the longest two hundred yards I've ever walked in my life. It was raining hard, and the wind was blowing even harder. Every step I took sank directly into six inches of mud, and then I had to yank myself out of it to take the next step forward. Halfway there I considered turning around and getting back on the bus. This shit was treacherous. But an idea had come to me, and I was determined to see it through.

I was going to find a Coupe de Ville and spray-paint a Spider-Man mask on the hood.

I had not drawn a Spider-Man mask since I was in

elementary school. But I knew how to do it. For me, drawing a Spider-Man mask comes as easy as signing an autograph. It's muscle memory. You know those little drawings you learn as a jit that you end up covering all your schoolbooks with? Like the "S" symbol that starts out with the two sets of three parallel lines. Do you guys know what I'm talking about? When I was in the second grade, a classmate of mine named Alex Chang taught me to draw a Spider-Man mask in a similar fashion. I went on to draw that shit a thousand times. Shout-out to Alex Chang, wherever he is today. That was my guy.

I can't tell you exactly why I wanted to lay down a Spider-Man at Cadillac Ranch. Maybe it had something to do with the idea of childlike wonderment that had been on my mind since my visit to the Barber Museum. Whatever the source of inspiration was, Spider-Man was the mark I wanted to leave there. It just came to me in that moment. That's just how it goes sometimes.

But as I approached the Cadillacs, it became clear that I would not be spray-painting my tribute to Alex Chang, or anything else for that matter. The cars were surrounded by mud puddles. I would be up to my knees in mud if I attempted this. I also realized that due to the winds, it would be impossible to achieve my Spider-Man even if I were to submerge myself in the mud baths. The spray paint would blow back into my face before it even touched one of these cars. The most likely outcome would be me getting back on the bus covered in mud from the waist down and neon paint from the waist up.

I tossed the can of paint into a puddle and headed back to the bus. Forgive me for littering at this national landmark. I don't condone littering. But I was frustrated. I had fought through the elements in order to reach that Coupe de Ville and leave my Spider-Man on it. To not be able to see it through was another punch to the gut. It seemed like this whole trip was snakebitten. I got on the bus and tossed my Air Forces in the trash.

As we got back onto the highway and started heading toward Santa Fe, I couldn't help but think we were on a dummy mission. Right now we were in Amarillo. There was an airport here. I could have my sister send the jet out and pick us up. It would take us straight to Las Vegas and I'd have an extra day to rest up before my show.

I was conflicted, because I still wanted to keep the road trip going and make it for the sweat lodge ceremony. But the longer we drove into this blizzard, the farther we'd be from an airport, and the more difficult our exit strategy would be. I did not want to fuck around and end up stuck in a massive storm and miss my show. It wasn't even about the money. I just didn't want to let down the thousands of people who had come to Sin City that weekend with plans of partying with Ricky Rozay.

I decided to call my sister and fill her in on the situation. But when I reached into my pocket for my phone, it wasn't there. Instead, I pulled out that small yellow card I'd gotten the night before.

> Stop worrying about what is beyond your control and start focusing on what is. Some things are just written in the stars, my friend. Now is the time to step back and watch your life unfold before your eyes. Some of the best things happen when you least expect it.

I shook my head. I didn't have time for Zoltar's shit right now.

At that moment, I felt my phone vibrate in the pocket of my hoodie. I was getting a call. It was Slab.

"Bro," he said breathlessly. "I'm flying into New Mexico for the sweat lodge ceremony so I can pray for my mother's passage. I land at one o'clock."

Slab was on his way.

In *The War of Art*, Steven Pressfield spends a lot of time talking about "Resistance." It's essentially the core concept of the book. In it, "Resistance" is used as a catch-all term that encompasses all of the evil forces—procrastination, self-doubt, perfectionism, to name a few—that keep us from completing our creative work. According to Pressfield, those forces become most powerful as artists approach the end of a creative endeavor.

"The danger is greatest when the finish line is in sight," he writes.

For the most part, Pressfield is referring to internal forces. At least, I don't think he had epic blizzards in mind when he was writing that. He does acknowledge the reality of external obstacles, but he says they only win if you give them power.

Whether or not I was going to make it to Santa Fe was out of my control. There was a strong likelihood the storm would get worse and Slab may have to partake in this ceremony by himself.

What was in my control was a choice I had to make. Was I going to fold on this experience before it folded on me?

Sixty seconds earlier, I was leaning in that direction. But after seeing Zoltar's note and learning Slab was already en route, I felt pulled the other way. I closed my eyes and waited for an answer to come to me.

In my mind's eye, I saw Elvis's Colt .45 that'd been on display at Graceland. The one with the custom turquoise grips. The one below the ID that was issued on the day I was born.

Turquoise is a cultural symbol of Santa Fe and the American Southwest. For centuries, Native American tribes have regarded the green-and-blue mineral as a sacred gemstone that represents protection, healing, and spiritual well-being. The region is home to some of the richest turquoise mines in the world and that natural abundance made it a central material in local arts and crafts.

Turquoise is also associated with the direction west. Which is where we were supposed to be going.

There were too many signs for it all to be a strange coincidence. These had to be messages from the universe.

I had to press forward toward Santa Fe. I had to make it to my renewal ceremony. This wasn't like Kilimanjaro. The pieces were all lining up. I had the vision and willpower to see this through.

I abandoned my plan to call my sister and abort the mission. I looked out the bus window and watched as snow started to fall from the sky. *Some things are just written in the stars, my friend. Now is the time to step back and watch your life unfold.*

"It's too easy, Slab. I'll see you in a few hours."

CHAPTER 18

WINTER STORM ANYA AND THE HOUSE OF HEAT

BY LATE MORNING, WE HAD REACHED THE point of no return. Interstate 40 had turned into a parking lot and our bus was at a standstill in the middle of a miles-long traffic jam.

We had missed our window of opportunity to safely reverse course. To attempt a U-turn now would have been a death wish. The deep, unplowed snow in the median made that basically impossible for any vehicle but even more so for a coach bus. What the fuck had I been thinking?

I had the benefit of only being a passenger on this bus. I sparked a joint and stared out the window. I was captivated by what I saw outside. Me being from Miami, I haven't seen a lot of snow to begin with. But this shit here? We're talking complete whiteout conditions. It was to a magnitude that was hard to fathom. There were downed trees and blown power lines. Jackknifed semitrucks, overturned rigs, and multi-vehicle pileups. National Guard Humvees and plow trucks. I was fascinated. We were in the Southwest United States in the first week of November. How was this possible?

For Buddy, I can only imagine that his excursion through Winter Storm Anya was a much more harrowing experience. I know he was up front leaning all the way forward in his seat, squinting out the windshield for the slightest bit of visibility. I know his defrosters were on full blast. I know he had to be white-knuckling that steering wheel. I wouldn't be surprised if that drive haunts Buddy for the rest of his days.

For better or worse, we had committed to slowly and dangerously pressing forward to Santa Fe. What was supposed to be a four-hour drive ended up taking us ten, and for those ten hours, I wasn't even worrying about what I was going to do if we didn't make it in time for the sweat lodge. I was worried about ending up getting stuck and stranded in some snowbank. I'd left all my furs and shearling coats back at home and was already down one pair of Air Forces.

But against all odds, somehow, some way, we made it.

I knew it hadn't happened by accident. This couldn't just be dumb luck. There had to have been a higher power that had protected and shepherded us through this storm. That supernatural force had tapped Zoltar to be the messenger, to encourage me to keep going. I became convinced it was my destiny to be in Santa Fe that night. This was no longer just a road trip. This had become a spiritual quest.

The snow was still falling, but it had slowed down considerably. So had the winds. When I stepped off the bus, it took me a minute to gather my bearings. My eyes had to adjust from the bright LED lighting inside to the quiet darkness of the night outside.

If there was a path I was supposed to go down, I couldn't see it. There was at least two feet of snow on the ground. I began my trek toward the only thing I could see: flickers of flame from a fire pit in the distance. As I got closer, I could see there were three figures in robes standing around the fire.

A few steps later, I realized one of them was Slab. My dawg really had on a robe and was standing around a bonfire surrounded by snow.

The two other individuals introduced themselves. Our spiritual guide was a local curandera (healer) named Concha, a seventy-five-year-old Zapotec from Oaxaca, Mexico. From the moment I laid eyes on Concha I knew this woman had a beautiful soul. She had an assistant with her, another lovely woman named Stacey, to help out with the ceremony. It was clear to me these women had no idea who I was.

"It's wonderful to meet you," I said. "I'm William."

"Have you ever experienced a sweat lodge?" Concha asked.

I shook my head.

She smiled.

"Well, you won't be able to say that again. I hear that you have traveled a long way to be here this evening. What brings you here? Do you have a personal intention for the ceremony?"

"I just want to learn about myself."

Ten feet from the fire pit was a small, dome-shaped

structure made of stone. This was where the renewal ceremony would be taking place. Before going in, Concha let us know a little bit about what we were getting into.

A temazcal renewal ceremony is a sacred Indigenous sweat lodge ritual. It symbolizes going into the womb of Mother Earth to renew oneself. The ceremony is conducted in four stages. Each "doorway" we'd enter was aligned with one of the four cardinal directions and four stages of life. Each one had its own season, element, medicine, and spirit animal to symbolize the energy of that phase.

"It is hot," Concha warned. "And once we close the doorway, it is pitch-black. Sometimes people can get uncomfortable, but there is a purpose in the discomfort. We say that when we are praying, when we're asking for renewal, we give up a little bit of our comfort to receive that blessing. The heat and the darkness are powerful medicines. I have seen some incredible realizations come to people in the darkness. When we can't use our sense of vision, we have to go inside and use our other senses."

Before entering the sacred space, Concha wanted to rid us of any spiritual weight we might be carrying. She lit some herbs and smudged our foreheads with the smoke, using a bird's feather. With that, we were ready to go inside.

"I just ask that when you enter the center doorway, you enter through the left. Follow your heart."

We followed her instructions and formed a seated circle around the heated stones in the center of the room.

There were benches on all sides, but Concha said we could move to the cooler floor if the heat got to be too much. Once we found our seats, Stacey closed the door and everything went pitch-black.

"I invite you to put your mind aside. Feel your back against the wall. Your butt on the chair. Feel the connection. Feel the warmth. Feel this black darkness holding you like a warm blanket. Envision yourself as a tiny, tiny seed in the warm loving waters of Mother Ocean. Newly conceived. By magic. By love. Feel the warm waters rocking you. Nourishing you. Loving you. Just as when you were in the womb of your mother. That nourishment allows you to grow and become you."

In my forty-eight years of life, I had never heard anyone speak like this. These were not the type of things you grow up hearing in Carol City.

"A large mother turtle comes, and you land on her

back. And she carries you to the shores of Mother Earth, gently placing you on the sand. You take your first breath as a two-legged. You turn and you crawl and you walk into the first doorway. The doorway of the South. This is the place of your childhood. This is the place of your innocence. This is the place of magic. For no one needs to tell you that you can understand your four-legged friend. Or the butterfly that comes when you think of someone that you love."

I breathed in, focusing everything on visualizing her words as she continued.

"There's a deer prancing and dancing. It is your guide in the spirit world of the South. You are innocent, magical, and trusting."

Concha recited a Native prayer in a language I was not familiar with. But I could feel it.

"Oh, Creator. We're gathered here in this darkness. I ask that you touch my relatives here. That they might remember something inside of them. A sweet memory. An innocent memory. A trusting memory of their childhood. I'm thinking of my aunt. She told me that when she was four years old, she found herself up in the clouds, and that the clouds filled her hands with stars. And she was told that she would have a good life. When she told me this, she was ninety. I said, 'But Aunty, you had a really hard life.' And she said, 'Yes, but I always knew that it would be a blessing.'"

Concha had a rattle that served as a talking stick. After she shared a story, she would shake the rattle so the next person could "see" it with their ears and then pass it off to them. She passed it to Stacey, who spoke and then passed it to Joanne. Then to Neil. Then me. Then Slab.

I won't get into the specifics of everyone's personal stories. Much of what was shared that night will stay within those cedar walls. I'll just say that shit got real deep. Everybody leaned into the experience. *Vulnerability* is not the first word that comes to mind when you think of the biggest boss Rick Ross. Maybe it was the heat or our collective exhaustion from the journey to get there that day, but we all let our walls down.

"So on the count of three," Concha said, "we are going to say 'All My Relations.' I invite you to say it from the deepest part of you, because innately, in this darkness, we all know that we are all related. We feel it. We need the water. We need the air. We need the earth. We need the fire. All nations of this earth. You've got to say it from the deepest part of you . . . One . . . Two . . . Three. ALL MY RELATIONS!!!"

Without being able to see each other, we all shouted it at the top of our lungs. Nobody held back. It was pitch-black, but we all had our eyes wide open. It was as if we could see each other even when there was nothing there.

Then Stacey opened the door and a rush of cold air came in. My vision returned as the lodge's exterior lighting flowed into the space.

"Wow," Concha said. "I've never heard 'All My Relations' said so sincerely. That was incredible."

I looked around the room. Everyone was sweating

profusely. We rehydrated with a natural Gatorade—a homemade concoction of ice water, lemon, and salt. After we replenished all the water we were losing, Stacey closed the door and we were back in the darkness again.

From there, we entered the doorway to the West, where Concha invited us to imagine an encounter with a brown bear in the forest.

"In the West, we consider that bear a medicine bear. It knows which bark to pull off a tree to soothe that fever. It knows what roots to pull to soothe a sore throat. In this direction we ask for the medicines we may need in our lives. It might be something over the counter, or it might simply be asking to have better communication with a sibling or spouse."

The third doorway was the North, where, with Concha leading us forward, we came into contact with a wolf. The wolf symbolized the wisdom we had gained from others. We passed the rattle and shared stories about the wisdom we'd gained from ancestors, guides, leaders, and even our children.

The fourth and final doorway was to the East.

"Once again, put your mind aside," she instructed. "Feel with your heart. Feel with your feelings. And envision in the distance a tall tree. An evergreen. On top of the highest branch, there's the biggest and most beautiful eagle. I invite you not to see it or visualize it . . . I invite you to *be* the eagle. Feel your claws on that high branch. Feel the wind whipping at your feathers and through your eyes. You've never seen so far through those eagle eyes.

"The medicine of the East offers us that sun in the morning so that we can see and get up and put our feet on the earth and carry out our visions and dreams and prayers. The eagle gives us the courage and will to keep going even in hard times. The eagle gives you clarity. I invite you to look through those eyes and see over the earth into the next day, into the next year, and the years to come. What do you see? For yourself. For your loved ones. I invite you to, when you're ready, spread those wings and fly.

"Creator, once again, we come to you. I want to thank you for the many visions and prayers that you have manifested into miracles in my life. So many times I've come to you on my knees. Talking to you with that sacred tobacco, with that sacred cedar, with that copal. Offering you those prayers . . . Offering you that smoke. Having that faith that in your infinite wisdom you will answer my prayers and make a miracle.

"I visualize a place where we're not suffering from floods or tornados or tsunamis because we are taking care of Mother Earth. For our children and our children's children. I visualize them being happy. For my brothers and sisters who are here with me today, I ask that you make their visions a reality. I thank you for my life and I thank you for all my relations."

The rest of us shared our visions and then shouted "All My Relations" in unison one last time to bring the ceremony to its end. We had gone through all four doorways. We had completed the cycle of renewal and transformation. I lost all sense of time during this mystical experience, but it turned out we had been in that lodge for well over two hours.

I would've never thought I could spend two hours in that house of heat and darkness. But I'd been fully present and engaged the whole time. My thoughts had not strayed once. I pride myself on being a man of words, but at that moment I didn't have the vocabulary to do justice to what the experience had meant to me. I was grateful for Concha and Stacey, and I was grateful to have shared it with Slab, Neil, and Joanne. I was grateful for my life.

"Most Friday nights," I shared with the group, rattle in my hand, "I'm somewhere getting paid to party. That's what most of my Friday nights look like. But tonight I was brought here, and I know it wasn't by mistake."

I looked around the group, pausing to take it all in.

"I wasn't thinking about money or music or anything outside of here. I was thinking about my inner being, and my past self and my future self. I know now my relations have a bigger purpose for me and I understand and accept that. The way they placed me here, I know they're going to put me in another position to understand whatever it is I need to do next. Thank you for blessing us with this."

CHAPTER

19

A BOSS RENEWED

THE NEXT MORNING, WE WERE BACK ON THE road. For a third consecutive day I would be spending more than ten hours on this bus. Knowing it would be the last one made the drive go by a little easier. All things considered, I was feeling pretty good—surprisingly better than I had at the start of the road trip when I was fresh off that flight from Dubai.

The ride to Vegas went down without any of the theatrics of our epic quest to reach Santa Fe. After stopping for breakfast and getting something to eat, we huddled up on the bus and had a debrief of our sweat lodge experience. The spirit world was a beautiful place. We all wanted to come back soon. Maybe next time Concha would invite us to one of the traditional all-night ceremonies, which last from sunset to sunrise.

As we began to approach the bright lights of Las Vegas, I knew I had to switch gears.

It was Saturday night in the city of sin. Time for me to shift my thoughts from the spirit world. That was quite the mental adjustment: twenty-five hundred people had come out to see the biggest boss Rick Ross at Drai's, and I was going to give them what they came for. I put my party hat back on and got back to business. For

those of us on the bus, the show was a celebration of the journey we'd taken together.

We had ourselves a hell of a night.

My jet was waiting for me in the morning. When I got back to Miami that night I took a shower and then immediately knocked out. It was the best night of sleep I'd had in a long time.

The next morning, I felt fresh—dare I say, renewed. I got up early, grabbed a joint, and headed outside for my morning walk. I took some time out to reflect on the road trip. Had I gotten what I'd wanted out of the experience?

Had I solved my midlife crisis? Was I out of my creative rut?

I was most definitely coming home with some amazing memories and a ton of new ideas. I'd gotten to take a short break from Rick Ross and dive deeper into William. I felt immense gratitude for my life and the people in it. But was that enough? And what about the book?

I don't know if this book ended up being the prescriptive, how-to-be-creative manual my publisher had in mind. I'm not sure that's how creativity works. But this process did result in me creating something. Something I'm putting out into the world and that you're reading right now.

The story of how this book came to be is, of course, the whole story of the creative process. Both are transformative, at times unpredictable journeys, with moments of awe, inspiration, struggle, frustration, detours, and discovery. At the end of the day, I believe this book illustrates that process better than I could tell it to you in some advice guide.

When you shake things up and step outside your norm, you never know what you might discover, who you'll meet, and what doors it will open. At a minimum, just getting exposed to things outside your wheelhouse will give you new material to draw from when you return to whatever your real craft is. But at the end of the day, you just have to keep going, fight the snowstorm, and get up onstage—even if the lightning hasn't struck yet.

When I got back to the house I called my sister. She gave me a rundown of what I had scheduled on my calendar that week. Then I got into my car and headed to the studio, where I had my engineer eMIX waiting for me.

eMIX loaded up some beats and we started our usual process of running through them one by one. Like I mentioned earlier, I'm pretty picky when it comes to production. For every hundred beats I listen to, there might be five in there that I choose to revisit later.

Play the next one . . . Next one . . . Next one . . .

Remember how I stopped in front of the Picasso painting at the Estefans' house, and the remote-controlled Lotus replica at the Barber Museum, and Elvis's turquoise Colt .45 at Graceland? When I first entered the spaces that housed those items, there was so much to take in. That's what my beat submission inbox looks like. The way I had to start moving through those spaces until something grabbed my attention is the same way I sift through beats.

Next one . . . Next one . . . Run that one back.

Twenty minutes in, one of them had me. I had eMIX run it back from the beginning and listened to it straight through a few times. Like looking at a piece of art from a distance, I let the beat wash over me in its totality. I took in the overall ambience and absorbed its energy.

Start it over.

I listened to the beat a few more times, but now each time I isolated a different element. I'd listen to it while only paying attention to the drums. *Start it over.* Then the baseline. *Start it over.* Then the sample.

With the beat playing on a loop, I closed my eyes and let it marinate in my mind. A few minutes later, I started humming to myself. I was finding my pocket. Figuring out my flow.

I reached for my joint and took a deep inhale. I put it down and reached for my pen. I was ready to write again.

★ ★ ★ ★ ★